# AS GOD IS MY WITNESS

# AS GOD IS MY WITNESS

## CARL ROSENBERG

HOLOCAUST LIBRARY
*An imprint of the*
UNITED STATES HOLOCAUST MEMORIAL MUSEUM
WASHINGTON, D.C.

This reprint is published by the United States Holocaust Memorial Museum, 100 Raoul Wallenberg Place, SW, Washington, D.C. 20024-2126.

Copyright © 1990 Carl Rosenberg; reprinted 2000

Cover photos *(clockwise from top left):* USHMM, courtesy of National Archives; USHMM, courtesy of Ilana Skutecky Breslaw; USHMM; USHMM, courtesy of George Kadish; Archiwum Panstwowego Muzeum w Oswiecimiu-Brzezince; USHMM, courtesy of Instytut Pamieci Narodowej/Institute of National Memory; USHMM, courtesy of Coenraad Rood; USHMM, courtesy of Gedenkstaette Buchenwald. Title page photo: USHMM, courtesy of Archiwum Panstwowego Muzeum w Oswiecimiu-Brzezince. The cover photographs reflect events of the period and do not necessarily represent the author's personal experiences.

ISBN 0-89604-143-3

Typeset by Duke & Company, Devon, Pennsylvania
Printed by Victor Graphics, Inc., Crofton, Maryland

*Printed in the United States of America*

*For My Mother, Father, Sisters, and Brothers*


My Dear Mom and Dad:

It took me a very long time to fulfill my promise to you to write this Holy Memorial for you and your loved ones.

Your dream was that we would perhaps all survive the war, but that dream was shattered on September 1st 1939 when you were forced to die by those German vampires. You and Dad did not complain of your suffering and of the agony and heartbreak of witnessing the death of your children and the execution of your beloved son Moisze Szyja in March of 1943.

I have written this book in my own words so that the world will not forget the horrors of the Nazi regime.

As I said, it has taken me a very long time to write, but even after so many years my eyes are wet with sorrow and time will never heal the memories I have of my lost family. I am getting older and long for the day when we shall all be together again.

Your loving son,

Carl

# acknowledgments

Ed Bernstein for the photographs
Biographical cover photo: Chris Amato—Amato Color Labs, Omaha, Nebraska
My loving wife Rachel and the children, Annie, Maurice, and Stuart for their abiding support and patience
Captain David Nuttall for his inspiration, time, and for his encouragement and insistence that I complete the manuscript
Oliver Pollak for his invaluable input and time
Dr. Frank Hilf for his generous assistance
Julius Sax for his excellent research and support

**W**hen my father was courting my mother in Poland, he would walk twelve kilometers from his village of Przitick to hers. Sometimes he borrowed a horse and buggy, so he wouldn't have to walk. This was a time when the world was not as modern as it is now.

My mother and father both descended from Orthodox Jewish families. According to Jewish law, a woman was required to cut off all her hair when she got married. But the night before her wedding, my mother rebelled. She told her parents she would not cut off her hair. "What do you mean?" they asked her. "It's against the Law." But she told them she didn't care, that she wouldn't do it, even if it meant not getting married. Her parents took her to the rabbi and explained the problem. The rabbi said to them, "If she doesn't want to cut off her hair, don't force her." He told them she could wear a wig for the wedding, as if she had cut off her hair, then she could remove it afterwards. So my mother put on the wig and got married. After that day, none of my mother's sisters cut their hair when it was their turn to wed.

◆ ◆ ◆

After my parents married, they lived in my mother's village of Wolanow. My father's skin was darker than the other Jews in the village, because he was descended from a long line of Sephardic Jews who had left Spain around 1350 and finally settled in Poland. His father had been a blacksmith who had become famous for inventing a new kind of metal plow that became the standard one in eastern Europe. Even though my grandfather had invented it, he worked for a wealthy landowner, and this man took all the credit for the invention. He had the plow mass-produced, and never gave grandfather even a part of the proceeds. Grandfather died of cholera during an epidemic in 1895, when my father was only seven years old.

My father grew up on a farm that belonged to Polish landowners. He knew everything about farming and was an expert on orchards. He rented them from Polish farmers and would tend the trees and harvest the fruit for my mother to sell. In the winter he would borrow a sled from a friend, and my brothers and sisters and I would ride into the woods to watch him chop down a tree and cut it into pieces for the fire.

Wolanow was a very small village. There were only about 300 people in all, maybe 200 Jews and the rest Christians. The Jews who lived in Wolanow were butchers, blacksmiths, shoemakers, and other artisans. We lived in a small house with one large room with a wooden floor, on which we all slept and ate. In one corner, my father had a workshop for making new shoes and repairing old shoes. There was no indoor plumbing or running water. We had to fetch water in buckets from a well in the center of the village, and for a toilet we used a pot. We had a woodstove for heat and for cooking, and we had a cow for milk. I remember the wonderful aroma of the bread that mother baked every day. I also remember the beautiful farmlands and orchards that I could see from our house.

Every morning my father would rise very early, about five A.M., and work on shoes in his corner of the room until almost six. From our beds we could watch him working by the light of a kerosene lamp. At six, he went to pray and study Torah with the morning minyan. There was no synagogue in Wolanow, so a room in one family's house served as the synagogue. That was where we had prayers on Saturdays and holidays and where my father went every morning to study and pray. When he returned, our mother gave us a breakfast of bread, cheese, milk, sometimes cottage cheese, and chicory coffee. We couldn't afford to have meat more than once or twice a week, usually on Saturdays, so for lunch and dinner we would have potatoes, macaroni, kasha, or beans. Our parents earned enough so that we all had a healthy diet, and even though we weren't wealthy, our lives were, all in all, pretty good.

During the First World War, the Austrian army had invaded Poland and occupied Wolanow. At that time, I was two and my sister Rachel was four; our sister Toba was just a baby. My brothers Nathan David and Maurice were not born until after the war. At the time our house stood next to the Austrian army gendarme station. I remember that our parents were often out during the day. Father went out to get supplies, take orders, and pick up and deliver shoes, while mother sold farm produce door-to-door. Sometimes when our parents were gone, Toba would cry, and her crying would make the gendarmes' commandant furious. He would bang on our door with a huge piece of wood, shouting in German. We couldn't understand what he was shouting, and Toba would cry even more. I was afraid the commandant would break in and do something terrible to us. We already knew how the gendarmes could hurt people. Through the wall, we would sometimes hear men and women screaming in agony. Then we would hide in a dark corner of the room or underneath a table until our parents came home.

One day the Austrians left. The Polish army arrived in the area, and told us that the war was over. Although I was only five years old, I remember the relief supplies we received from America. For the first time in a long while, we had enough to eat.

Even though the war was over, I knew my father wasn't happy. He would tell us stories he had heard of Polish soldiers and Christian civilians roaming the streets and beating up Jews. He warned us to stay close to home because we might be attacked. We obeyed him. We didn't know it at the time, but we had just received our first lesson in "how to survive if you're Jewish in Poland." It was simple: stay out of sight, try to be inconspicuous for a while, and hope that the danger would pass. I would later learn that there was a catch to this rule: it didn't always work. At the time, we were only children and didn't understand such things. But, as time passed, I noticed a worried look appearing on my father's face more and more often.

When I was eight, we moved from the house next to the gendarme station to one owned by Eleksander Jakubowski, a man whose greatest joy in life was to tease me. Whenever he saw me on the street, he would pick me up by the ears and then drop me in a heap. Being lifted this way hurt, in fact it hurt a lot, and I was bothered by the smile on Eleksander Jakubowski's face whenever he made me suffer. I soon learned to recognize the sound of his footsteps and his voice and to tell whether he was headed in my direction. If he was, I would scoot away before he had a chance to grab me. If he were alive today, I would thank him for the little fun he had with me. Because of him I developed a "sixth sense" for anticipating danger. We were only playing "cat and mouse" games, at the time, but habits one picks up when young stay with you and, in my case, would save my life many times.

Slowly, Poland recovered from the war. Business improved and so did the living conditions. My father thought the anti-Semitism would stop, but instead, attacks against Jews were getting worse. It became obvious that most of the

Christians in our area believed Jews were inferior human beings. Some thought we weren't even human. I heard Christians talking to Jews and calling them "dirty Jews" or "Turks" or "Gypsies." In Radom, the largest city in our district, I saw groups of young men rioting in the streets and shouting, "Jews out of Poland! Go back to Palestine!"

In school it was no different. By law, all children in Poland had to be educated. Jewish families could send their children to Jewish schools, but there were none in Wolanow. Some of those Jewish families had their children tutored at home. But most of them never learned to speak Polish well—they were fluent in Yiddish and Hebrew only. As a result, they became even more isolated from the surrounding Christian community. In our home, things were different. Even though our parents were Orthodox Jews, they insisted that we go to public school to learn to speak, read, and write Polish just like the Poles. While our parents spoke Yiddish, Hebrew, and Polish, they could read and write only in Yiddish and Hebrew. They wanted their children to be literate in all three languages. So, during the day we went to public school where, along with our other lessons, we studied Polish and German. Afterwards, at night, my brothers and I would go to a *cheder,* a room in the home of a young Jewish teacher, to study religion, Yiddish, and Hebrew. The boys would all crowd into one half of a big room that served as our classroom and which was furnished with tables and benches. The other half, separated by a curtain, was our teacher's living quarters. He had a young daughter of about seven, and she would also sit in on our lessons.

By the time I was ten, I had developed a reputation as a very good student. However, this could be a mixed blessing. Many of the Christian children were jealous, and they insulted me and called me names, just as their parents did to Jews on the street. In school, the Christian students constantly picked fights with the Jewish ones, who they thought were weak and unable to defend themselves. One day I decided that it was time to teach these bullies a lesson. I recruited a few of the other Jewish students and we practiced fighting. Then we ambushed a group of the worst Christian bullies on their way home after school and gave them a dose of their own medicine. We were so successful that the next day the principal called my parents in to school and told them that I had been suspended for a couple of days. I thought this was strange because none of the Christian students were ever suspended or reprimanded when they beat Jewish boys. Then I thought that maybe this wasn't so strange after all. It was just the way things were. Christians always got special treatment, while Jews had to defend themselves in the best way they could. I also felt that this was wrong, it was unfair and needed to be changed.

Even though this was a public school, the Roman Catholic Church exerted a strong presence, and a priest taught catechism classes during the school hours. Jewish children were supposed to leave the classroom during catechism, but I was naturally curious, so one afternoon I stayed. When the priest entered the room all of the other children knelt and kissed his hand. I wasn't about to genuflect or kiss anyone's hand, so I remained in my seat. The priest was stunned. This was the first time he had ever had a "heretic" in any of his classes. After scolding me, he asked why I had behaved so poorly. I told him that I was Jewish and that, "We don't do all that kissing and kneeling." The priest was furious and slapped my face.

I kept attending the catechism class, however, because I was curious about this Catholic religion that was so different from ours. One day, after I had been going to the class for a few weeks, I was standing outside along with the other students, when the priest arrived. The other students took off their caps, but I didn't. This time the priest really lost his temper. In front of the other children, he grabbed my cap and threw it away, calling me a "dirty Jew."

This priest's attitude was no different from that of many of my teachers. The females were good to me and treated me like any other student, but the male teachers often insulted me because I was Jewish.

One of my teachers was also the school's principal. This man was very strict, and he liked to think of himself as the absolute ruler of the school. His word was law, and he would punish students any time he wanted. He had two assistants, a teacher and a governess whose job it was to make sure we were well behaved.

The principal lived in the schoolhouse, and, when it was cold, he had the boys carry wood from a storage depot to the school. In 1925, when I was ten years old, we had a very bad winter. It was so cold that the temperature sometimes went down to 15 or 20 degrees below freezing. Every day, six boys were assigned to carry wood to the school. It was a twenty-minute walk, and the bundles were heavy. The boys who were selected would start out for school at least an hour earlier than usual to make sure the wood arrived before classes began. To do so meant leaving home at 6:30 in the morning. A student who was late finishing the wood-carrying chore would be punished, sometimes by being forced to bend over a bench to be paddled in front of all the other students. The girls in the school were never whipped; their punishment was to kneel in the corner for fifteen to thirty minutes.

Normally, each of us had to carry wood twice a week, but one week after I had already carried wood three times, I was chosen once again. At that point, I refused. I told my teacher that I had been treated unfairly, and that I suspected the reason I was selected so often was that the female student who helped with the assignments was against Jews. But none of my pleadings did any good. I was whipped, and not by the teacher, which would have been humiliating enough, but by another student. I knew that I was being unjustly punished only because I was Jewish.

One summer, when I was eleven, the well at the school dried up and a new one had to be dug. The principal asked my brother Maurice and me if we wanted to earn some money carrying water from the central well in Wolanow to the schoolhouse. We took the job and went back and forth with the water every day until the new well was in operation. We took this money and bought used school books. I remember the scene at the village well, how the women used to compliment us on how handsome and strong we were. And that was true. All of my brothers and sisters were not only bright but also very handsome and beautiful.

◆ ◆ ◆

Once a Gentile family invited me for breakfast. The woman of the house asked me why Jews drank only milk and ate boiled eggs and bread for breakfast but didn't eat pork. I thought she was worried about how my diet might affect my health, so I assured her that I was healthy and that the reason I didn't eat pork was because it wasn't kosher.

Her husband started asking me why Jews were "that kind of people." He said, "What kind of religion lets people believe in such things as pork being forbidden for breakfast?" I was just about to explain what I knew about Jewish dietary rules when he started an anti-Semitic diatribe, stating that Jews obviously had a faith which bore a strong resemblance to that of dogs in the street. He said that the Jewish faith was no faith at all, unless animals had a faith. His anger and bitterness were chilling. The man's brother-in-law tried to calm things down by telling me that although the man owed me an apology, I shouldn't be offended because he didn't realize what he was saying. Then I told everyone that as far as I knew Jews were God's chosen people, and that we believed in the laws as Moses gave them, that it was obvious that the Jewish religion was not "a dog's belief." Getting in the last word made me feel better, but I knew it wouldn't change the man's hatred. Just like my anti-Semitic teacher, the priest who taught catechism, the Christian boys in my school who picked on Jews, and all the other Christian Poles who ridiculed Jews in the streets, this man's prejudices were part of the Christian Polish culture of the day. Many Poles didn't even know that Jesus was a Jew, a fact that the Catholic church in Poland apparently took pains to keep from them.

◆ ◆ ◆

When I was 13 years old, I decided to become a tailor. My uncle, Aron Waksberg, owned a tailor shop where he made and altered suits for private clients, and he offered to teach me the fundamentals. Then in 1933, when I was

18, I moved to Warsaw to work with another uncle who was also a tailor. Abram Blumenstien gave me free room and board and some money in return for my work. After a year, I had saved enough to bring my whole family to Warsaw. I enrolled in an evening trade school that taught advanced techniques in the art of clothes design, and there I perfected my skills in designing clothes, cutting fabrics, and other technical matters related to tailoring.

During the years that I studied tailoring, Polish anti-Semitism was growing more violent and widespread. Almost every day Jews were beaten or killed. These incidents became so commonplace that most Christians no longer paid any attention to them.

One Saturday evening in Radom a group of young Polish anti-Semites began rioting in the streets, beating any older Jews they encountered. Some of my Jewish friends and I went to help the victims. The fight was vicious, and I was injured when a fist caught my throat. Finally, we had to run or we would have been killed. For six weeks thereafter I could barely speak. Before the melee I had a good singing voice, but after that injury it never returned to its former quality.

By the time I finished my courses in tailoring I had already received a less formal education in languages and in survival. I was now fluent in four languages: Yiddish, Hebrew, Polish, and German. I had learned the art of street fighting and could defend myself, if necessary. I had also become interested in Zionism, because of some of my own experiences working in Warsaw, for workers' rights.

For a time while I was in Warsaw I was employed during the day by a tailor who was always late in paying my wages. Once he was six weeks in arrears, and when he finally did pay me it wasn't for the full amount. I demanded that I be paid weekly, like everyone else. When he refused I quit, but every day I returned to the shop to warn those responding to his "help wanted" advertisement how poorly he treated his workers. Finally, because no one would take the job, he was forced to pay me. I had my money, but I was still out of work.

Because I didn't look particularly Jewish, it was easier for me to get a job in the Christian section of the city, and I went to work for a man named Joseph Bromberg who was Jewish also and ran a tailor shop on Hoża Street. Joseph Bromberg was a successful tailor, and he was popular with a number of businessmen and government officials. After I had worked for him for a while, he placed more and more trust in me. Eventually he made me his assistant.

I helped him manage the shop and was also in charge of "customer relations," meaning that I would spend a lot of time talking with customers, either in the shop or on the phone. Telephones were rare in those days and very expensive, but the shop's clients were rich Christians, and many had phones. So, in spite of the cost, Bromberg had a telephone installed in the shop.

Among these customers were some very prominent men. General Slavoy Skladkowski, who was Interior Secretary and Secretary of Justice, and his family were regular customers, as were Joseph Beck, the Secretary of State, and Marshal Joseph Pilsudski. A number of newspaper editors were also patrons. Business was good and, although I was only twenty, I was making lots of money. I also was learning how to communicate with wealthy, powerful Christians, to make sure they were pleased with our work, and to encourage their loyalty to the shop and to me.

# chapter 2

When I was twenty-one I was drafted into the Polish army. Right after Passover, in May of 1937, I was assigned to the 34th Regiment, Biala Podlaska, Infantry. Of the two hundred and twenty men in my rifle company, thirty were Jews.

During the early days of basic training, the instructors were openly hostile to Jews. It was quite evident that they didn't like us and didn't want us there, but under the constitution of Poland, we were equal citizens. The concept of equal treatment for everyone, however, escaped most of our military superiors, and they did their best to make life difficult for us.

One Jewish soldier, Berek Goldberg, was an Orthodox rabbi who spoke little Polish because he had never attended the public schools. His father was the dean of a yeshiva on the outskirts of Warsaw. Berek was a misfit in the army and never should have been inducted. Because of his kosher diet, he couldn't eat the food served from the military kitchens. Instead, I would get him bread, kosher salami, and hard cookies, and an Orthodox woman from Biala Podlaska brought him kosher food that he would eat at lunchtime, sitting on the grass.

As was true of most Orthodox rabbis in Poland at that time, Berek had never done any strenuous physical work, and, as a result, he had a terrible time with his military training. In the army, where physical abilities counted for every-thing and brains for nothing, Berek couldn't even hit the targets during rifle practice. One day while on a march, we had to jump over a ditch. Berek fell and broke his leg and ended up in the hospital. It would have been better for him and the army if they had discharged him then. Instead they kept him in the hospital until his leg healed and then returned him to our unit.

Every morning Berek would put on his tallis and tefillin and he would pray. The Gentile soldiers would make fun of him and even throw things at him or kick and push him around while he was praying; he had become the company's scapegoat. Finally, I told him that I would stand guard while he prayed. I held a piece of lumber in my hand and threatened to attack anyone who tried to harass him. Berek was grateful and did what he could do best to reciprocate. He said prayers for me. He told me, "Carl, if I pray in the morning I will have done my daily *mitzvah*. For every mitzvah I perform a mark is placed in God's accounting books. It's like a bank account. The more mitzvahs, the bigger the account. So now I will assign half of them to you so when you die you'll have a good sized account."

A few weeks later a Jewish chaplain, Rabbi Stern, was assigned to our regiment. The rabbi organized a *minyan,* a twenty-minute prayer period, for the Jewish troops in the 34th Regiment, every morning at five. Berek was so excited, he looked like the happiest person in the world. Rabbi Stern told us that we could break the dietary rules because we had "no choice" of the food they offered us in the army. That made many of us feel better, although Berek still wouldn't eat the army food.

Unlike Berek Goldberg, I did fairly well in the army. Although I didn't care for life as an army private, I had no interest in suffering needlessly, and I made up my mind to become as proficient as I could in military skills. I became a good marksman and trained as a sharpshooter.

My scores on the written tests qualified me for advanced training that, under normal circumstances would have been the first step towards promotion to warrant officer in military intelligence. But before starting the training, I had to declare my religion on the application, Catholic, Jewish, Russian Orthodox, Lutheran, or whatever. I stated that I was Jewish, and my application was rejected.

My commanding officer told me that I could go to school and become a corporal, but, becoming an officer in military intelligence was out of the question. The implication was that I had declared myself to be Jewish and that did not help to advance one's military career. So I made up my mind that I would finish my service and go on to something else. I fulfilled my military obligation, and, in the fall of 1938, I returned to Warsaw and to Bromberg's tailor shop on Hoża Street where I worked until the spring of 1939.

In March of 1939 some of the army reservists were called up. It wasn't a general mobilization, but rather a quiet recall of reservists who were born in 1914 and 1915. Poland was preparing for a Nazi invasion. At that time, I was living at home with my parents, my two brothers, and two sisters. One morning a messenger arrived with instructions that I was to report to the 13th Infantry Regiment at Pultusk, a city with a large Jewish population 100 kilometers north of Warsaw.

In the 13th Regiment the anti-Semitism was worse than it had been during my earlier army service in the 34th. Christian soldiers would regularly kick and hit us while on maneuvers or on a march. I remember that once, as I was washing canteens, a soldier whose parents were Germans living in Poland hit me in the back, taking me completely by surprise. I was so angry at this unprovoked attack that I hit him over the head with the canteen I was washing and punched him on the nose. The MPs came, and I was taken to the officer in charge, but after I told him what had happened and how I had to defend myself, he dismissed me without any punishment.

Another time while on duty in Pultusk, several of us Jews were standing with some Christian soldiers. I remember that we were near the most modern building in the camp. Somehow a fist fight started. Several of us were from Warsaw, including one fellow named Golombek. He ordered all the Jews to move into a corner room, where we readied our rifles to defend ourselves. Golombek wasn't going to allow another soldier to beat him up. The fight quickly developed into a riot. The corporal on duty called the duty officer who arrived on the scene with a dozen gendarmes. The MPs blew their whistles, and the riot ceased almost at once. The duty officer listened to our story, and we were allowed to call our rabbi. Somehow the fight between the Christian and Jewish soldiers never received any further attention.

In June of 1939 we were released from active duty, but we were called up again in August when virtually all of the reservists were called in a general mobilization. I was ordered to report to the Warsaw Citadel, a fortress located on the river Vistula. Uniforms and other supplies were scarce, and many of us had to wear our civilian clothing for a few days until enough uniforms arrived. Then we were issued rifles and field equipment and were grouped into companies for deployment.

One of my first assignments was to patrol the streets of Warsaw. The officers asked for volunteers from the city who knew their way around. We were going to defend bridges and other strategic places such as ammunition depots in the event the Germans attacked. At that time, Poles of German descent were committing sabotage by blowing up ammunition and arms factories and depots as well as bridges. They were also helping German paratroopers who were being dropped over the forests near the cities. We were ordered to shoot anyone who looked suspicious and who wouldn't respond to our orders.

To prepare for a German assault, we began digging trenches. We conscripted young men and even boys to help us. The Christian soldiers picked Orthodox Jewish boys of twelve or thirteen years of age from the streets. They were easy to identify by their long, curled sideburns and yarmulkes. They were forced to work until they were exhausted. For many of them, two or three hours was all that they could physically manage. Occasionally, I was in charge of the work details, and then I tried to even things up by releasing the Jewish boys and rounding up some Christians.

On the first of September the Germans attacked Poland. They began with heavy bombing raids on Warsaw. By the 7th of September the German land forces had reached the outskirts of Warsaw.

My parents were living at 33 Nowolipke Street, and every day, after finishing my army duties, I still went home to eat dinner with them. One day my father said to me, "Carl, I want to go with you, and I want to bless you because you are going away to fight a war." He spoke of protecting the country and of my responsibilities as a soldier. "But never kill an innocent person," he said. In accordance with Jewish tradition, he placed his hand on my head and blessed me. Then my mother kissed me, and my father and I took a streetcar back to the gates of the Citadel. By the time we reached there he was almost in tears.

My father was a bearded, Orthodox Jew, and I was in uniform. The difference in our appearances was not lost on the soldiers who were passing by. A hooligan Christian soldier saw my father with his beard and demanded, "Are you a Jew? What are you doing here?" I told him to be quiet, that he was insulting my father and that he had no right to verbally abuse him. I started to fix the bayonet on my rifle, but my father told me to relax. The incident passed and my father kissed me goodbye. I stood there and watched as he boarded the streetcar to return home.

Eight days later we were ordered to the outer edge of the city facing the German lines, and we took up our positions in the trenches. We thought we were ready for them. I was given a portable machine gun that could be moved almost as easily as a rifle. My position was on the south side of the city, about seven blocks from where my Aunt Rose and Uncle Abraham Blumenstein lived with their children at 53 Grzybowska Street.

One day my Uncle Abraham saw me and came over to talk. He was obviously very hungry as there was a shortage of food, particularly among Jews. I gave him some extra bread I was carrying. I told him to return home because it was dangerous to walk in the streets, particularly near the trenches where a lot of inexperienced young soldiers were ready to shoot at anything that moved.

Sometime later, my father came to visit me. He spoke to the sentry on duty and asked if he could see his son, Carl Kiwa Rosenberg. The soldier told him to wait. When I finished my duties, I took my father into the building where I lived with the rest of my unit. I gave him bread, and we began to talk about what was happening to Poland. I remember he was crying. He was very worried about the danger I was in as a soldier fighting the Germans. My other two brothers had also been drafted and we both knew there was a good chance that all three of us might be killed. We were able to talk for a while, and before he left I gave him a few cans of food and several cigarettes.

# chapter 3

That night I was on duty in the trenches at the perimeter of the Polish lines. The trench was just large enough so that I could touch both sides by standing in the middle and stretching my arms out fully. I was supposed to be ready with a machine gun, but I was tired, and I dozed off for just a moment. I probably held my head in my hands while leaning against my machine gun. While I was doing this, I dreamed that my maternal grandfather, Jacob, was standing above the trench, in front of me towards the right. I reached out to touch him with my hand. As I did this, he said to me in Yiddish, "Kiwa, you have a very hard road to travel, but don't be afraid. Go ahead and be brave and remember I will watch out for your safety on your journey." I thought I could touch him because I felt certain he was standing there on the ground. At that instant, I awoke and found myself facing the duty officer who was checking the trenches to be sure all the soldiers were alert. He asked me if I was awake, and I assured him that I was. He told me to remember that sleeping on duty in wartime was punishable by death. That was all he said, and he moved on. As soon as the officer walked away from me, my thoughts returned to my dream.

My grandfather had been an Orthodox Jewish butcher who had four sons and four daughters. He would carry the meat on his back and sell it from house to house. I don't know why I should have dreamed about him in the trenches, but his prophecy of the hard road I was to travel and his promise to protect me, I recalled many times in the years that followed.

During this time Stefan Starzynski, Warsaw's mayor, tried to maintain order. He told the civilian population of Warsaw to help the soldiers in any way they could. He even urged wives to go and fight alongside their husbands, if they could find them. Starzynski told the people to continue with their daily activities as if no war was being fought. He spoke on the radio and told the people to go to the market because the pigs had arrived. "Help the butchers there," he said. "Go personally to the post office and pick up your mail. The banks are open, so do your banking. All the stores must be kept open."

I could never understand how he could say things like that and expect people to believe him. The German bombers were passing over the city every hour, sometimes even more often, and they were firebombing all parts of the city. The artillery fire picked up where the bombers left off.

There were fires everywhere, and they were worst in the Jewish sections of the city that were not protected by the fire department, the police, or the army. I saw people running out of burning houses, trying to save themselves. Hospitals and children's homes were also attacked. I remember seeing patients from one bombed hospital crawling on all fours trying to escape the flames. The Jewish childrens hospital was also in flames, but the Christians in charge of fire fighting did little to save the children. All of Warsaw had become an inferno. To make matters worse, the bombing had cut off the water supply and electricity. The city was paralyzed.

Two days after my dream, we received orders to attack the Germans, but it was too late. They had already begun the process of surrounding Warsaw. Early one morning, at about 7:30, we started moving into a tomato field, about one thousand meters long. Holding our rifles before us, we walked into the field in lines, one following another. The Germans had dug trenches at the other end of the field and were quietly watching us as we slowly moved towards them. Then they began shooting, just a few shots at a time. Even though there weren't many bullets at first, a few of the soldiers halted in their tracks, terrified of being hit. When that happened, officers would beat them with the wooden canes they carried, shouting, "Keep moving! Keep moving! Get to the front!" I was especially vulnerable because I didn't have a helmet. There had been a shortage of helmets and our officers had decided, in the finest Polish tradition, not to give them to Jewish soldiers for as long as there was a shortage.

All of a sudden the bullets came so thick that many of our contingent began to fall after being hit. Someone who was walking right next to me fell dead. I quickly grabbed his helmet and put it on. I was shaking with fear, and the men around me looked frightened to death. I lay down flat on the ground and dug a little mound of earth in front of my head for protection. Most of the other soldiers did the same thing, and many were so scared that they wet or soiled their pants. After fifteen minutes of lying on the ground we were ordered to fix our bayonets. Then we were told to run forward, while screaming, "Hurrah, hurrah!" It was straight out of World War I—the infantry trying to storm the trenches. And the results were the same: the charging infantry was slaughtered by machine-gun fire.

As I ran, I noticed that most of our troops were falling, dead or wounded. Those of us who were still unhurt lay down again. By this time we were pretty close to the Germans, and I could see a bunker a hundred or so meters away. From inside, three heavy machine guns were spitting out a stream of bullets. I could see the flames from the guns, and I thought: "They will kill us all." So I told the soldier lying next to me to go back and get a message to our light artillery, giving them the coordinates of the bunker. Ten minutes later the artillery knocked out the bunker with only three shots.

With the machine guns out we could move forward again. We ran towards the Germans, throwing hand grenades, many of which landed in the trenches. The Germans were forced to retreat and did so, again in the classic World War I manner—they just ran back through the network of trenches.

We ran forward and leaped into the abandoned German trenches, in the safety of which, we could rest. The Polish infantry had been divided into two groups. The right and the left wings. I was in the left wing. I could still hear gunfire and see puffs of smoke from the area where the right wing was fighting. As for the left, I could see that in my company only ten of the original 240 were still able to fight.

All of a sudden we heard the buzz of an airplane engine. It was a German observation plane. We were tempted to shoot at it, but someone shouted, "Don't shoot—it will give away our position." About a half hour later—after the German artillery had time to plot the coordinates that the pilot of the observation plane had given them—an artillery barrage was aimed precisely at where our right wing was fighting. We could see the entire group being destroyed by the exploding shells. Arms, legs, and heads went flying through the air like parts of toy soldiers, and in ten minutes, hundreds of men who had been fighting on our side were dead. It became very quiet.

We waited in the trenches until a noncommissioned officer came over to our group and told us to retreat. The few of us remaining on the left got out of the trenches and walked backwards through the tomato field, every now and then shooting our rifles in the direction of the Germans until we were past the field.

Then we were able to turn around and start back in the direction of Warsaw. Soon we ran into several companies of air force troops who were now being used to help the army defend the city. They were under the command of a captain who, when he saw that we were heading away from the front, started screaming at us, "What's the matter, why are you running away from the battlefield?" We told him we had been ordered to retreat, but he told us to return to the front line, and attack the Germans again. He was quite adamant and was not going to take no for an answer, so I told him that if he was so eager to attack the Germans he should take his air force troops and fight as much as he wanted, but we were in the regular army and we didn't have to listen to his orders.

By then it was late in the afternoon. We continued heading back towards Warsaw, but it began to get dark, and we were near a mine field, so we decided to stop for the night. In the morning the air force captain found us, and he ordered us to go with him to the command headquarters. He was very insistent, so we obeyed. There, to my surprise, we were placed under arrest as "deserters." Several officers began interrogating us. While my fellow soldiers were scared to death and wouldn't say anything, I told the questioners about the noncommissioned officer who had passed along the order to retreat and that, if they asked him, he would corroborate our story. This NCO had been with us until we were arrested. He had been a friend of one of the military policemen who held us in custody and who, we found out, had ordered him released. Now he was nowhere to be found. Because of this mix-up we were facing death by firing squad as deserters.

But the army was losing and had more need for experienced combat troops than for dead "examples" that would scare the other soldiers into marching to certain death before the muzzles of blazing machine guns. So the officer in charge told us that we would not be shot but instead, would be sent back to the front lines. The front lines turned out to be a network of deep trenches with several inches of water at the bottom. We were in one set of trenches, and the Germans were in another, a few hundred yards away. I could see them popping their heads up to get a look at us, and they could see our soldiers doing the same thing. This went on for a few days. Then things changed. The Germans began to shoot at anyone they could see. Most of our troops had been drafted recently and were inadequately trained. They were still trying to get a good look at the Germans by raising their heads, and a good percentage of those who did this were quickly shot dead. The others soon learned to keep their heads down.

I had been given two portable machine guns (similar to the American Browning Automatic Rifles) and a lot of magazines of ammunition. I set up the guns, placing the barrels through a groove in the ground, through which I could also see the German positions. I would only shoot one gun at a time; the other was my spare. When the Germans would start shooting I would return fire, aiming my gun towards the top of their trenches, and pulling the trigger while slowly rotating the gun from right to left until the barrel got red hot. Then I would set that one aside and use the other. The effect was to spray bullets over the trenches, the same thing they were doing to us. This little game lasted for approximately a week.

The conditions were terrible. We had to live in a muddy trench all the time. It seemed like a stalemate between the two armies, with the soldiers sitting in the cold, damp trenches indefinitely. Then one day the Germans attacked. Looking through my observation slit I could see hundreds of Germans climbing over the edge of their trenches, starting to run towards us. I had an assistant who helped me load ammunition magazines into my gun. I just kept the gun aimed at the closest group of Germans and fired. After a few minutes, when one gun got too hot, I fired the other one. The German troops didn't fare too well. Many were falling, and finally those who remained had enough sense to retreat to the safety of their trenches. A few days later the Germans tried another attack, and again our machine-gun fire drove them back. We were beginning to feel that we had faced the Germans, and that they weren't invincible.

Several days later, early in the morning, we were told that at ten A.M. we were to stop shooting, that a cease-fire had been negotiated with the Germans. At ten we heard bugles from both sides. The playing lasted for fifteen minutes, during which time we could still hear an occasional shot off in the distance.

We held our position for about twenty-four hours after the cease-fire. Some of the commanding officers from the field gathered the surviving members of the regiment for singing and prayers. We sang Polish national songs, and we all wept, from the highest officer to the lowest-ranking enlisted man. We cried not only because the Germans had beaten us, but also because we knew that the best treatment the Germans were likely to offer us wouldn't be good, and the worst was likely to be so bad that we didn't even want to think about it.

According to the terms of the surrender, the officers were to place themselves directly under German control. We enlisted men were told that eventually we would be able to go home. So we laid down our weapons and left the battle area. I met two girls who lived near my parents' house, and I asked them to tell my parents that I was all right. We picked tomatoes, potatoes, carrots, and turnips from a field, and the girls took them home after assuring me that they would let my family know that I was alive and well.

Then the Germans arrived. The first ones we saw were in tanks and armed with machine guns. Then the foot soldiers arrived and ordered my company, along with several others, to form a group for the long march to the Polish army camps of Kutno-Lowicz, about seventy-five kilometers from Warsaw. As we were marching, some of the German-speaking Polish officers talked with a German guard about Germany and Russia's plot to destroy Poland. The guard said that Germany planned to conquer France next and then England. During the march we received no food. Some of the men complained about how we were being treated. These men were taken away, and we never saw them again. I am sure that they were shot.

We were taken to a prisoner-of-war camp at Kutno-Lowicz. For two days we had no food or water. Then, on the third day the Germans gave us salted herring without water. Soon we were desperately thirsty. One of our men spotted a water faucet and crawled out under the wire to get a drink. Just as he turned the faucet on, one of the German guards shot him.

We were held at Kutno-Lowicz for five days. On the fifth day I was one of about one thousand enlisted men who were released. I began to walk towards Warsaw and was able to "hitch" a few rides by jumping on the backs of slow-moving German trucks without being seen by the drivers. I reached Warsaw after dark. There was so much devastation that I didn't recognize many of the streets. Danger was everywhere. There was a curfew and Germans patrolled the streets. By keeping a careful lookout, I was able to reach my parents' house safely. I was still in uniform and perhaps for that reason I was not stopped; I looked like just another Polish soldier. My parents were surprised to see me. My mother hugged me and began to cry, she was so happy to see me alive.

# chapter 4

When the Germans took control of Warsaw, they took twelve hostages, including Mayor Starzynski, scholars, and clergymen. They announced that they would shoot one or more hostages whenever a German was killed by Poles. Two of the hostages were Jews, Abraham Gepner, a businessman, who was chairman of the Jewish Merchants' Association of Poland, and Shmuel Zygelbojm, a leader of the Bund or Jewish Socialist Party. Other Jewish leaders offered themselves as hostages, but they were rejected. Under the rules of occupation, the Germans said that they would release the hostages if the population obeyed their orders. The population was generally compliant, but the German promises ultimately were lies. The mayor was taken away as a German prisoner. The Jewish hostages were released, but they were later arrested again and killed.

The Germans used the rules of occupation to justify their public hangings, which occurred almost every day. They also decided who could go in and out of Warsaw as well as all the towns surrounding the city. Then they began to seize Jewish property. We were in a panic. This was the first indication that we were going to be treated differently from the rest of the population.

Of course, there was a certain amount of resistance. I remember that some Christian women were very hostile to the German soldiers who were on the streets. A few spat in their faces. These women had not been molested or disturbed but were distraught by the German presence. It was their way of striking back, and it turned out to be a very costly one. The women were arrested and hanged. By that time we began to call the Germans the "modern Huns."

Every aspect of life was dangerous in occupied Warsaw, even my job as a tailor. Many of the shop's clients were now members of the German occupying forces, and they were demanding as well as dangerous. They spoke to Jews in the tailor shops in harsh and condescending tones. On several occasions tailors working with me were beaten by German clients who didn't like the way the clothes looked or because the tailor was late in finishing his work. One of the finest tailors in Warsaw, a friend of mine, opened a shop that specialized in making military uniforms. One day one of his clients, a German officer, didn't like the way the trousers of his new uniform fit. He took my friend outside, made him stand against a wall, and shot him. Another time, one of my own German clients pulled out a pistol and asked me if I knew what it was he was holding. I told him it looked like a gun. He told me I had better do a good job on his clothes or he would shoot me with it. So I had to be extremely careful to cater to my German clients' every whim to avoid being beaten or killed.

German placards were placed all over the city saying, "Labor and bread will be available to everybody," and "If orders are followed, no one will be harmed." Hitler visited Warsaw during the early weeks of the occupation. I remember his speaking in the central plaza at the famous Eleven Gates, a monument dedicated to Polish unknown soldiers of previous wars. The speaker's platform was blocked off from the general public, but everyone could hear Hitler' speech. Powerful loudspeakers carried his voice for several blocks. I remember Hitler saying that, "We have already achieved victory over our Polish enemy, and we are looking ahead to the defeat of the French and British."

Life for Jews was more difficult than for Christians, but no one had it easy. Christians and Jews alike were picked up off the street at random, arrested, and executed for things they hadn't done. Prominent Jewish leaders were also seized. Lawyers, doctors, and professors were taken away at night, never to be seen or heard from again.

All the while, the torture of the Jewish population became worse. Every day, even before the ghetto was fully enclosed, Jews were beaten and murdered in the streets. It was even dangerous for Jews to stop and talk on the street. The Germans patrolled the area in "volkswagens," jeeps with machine guns mounted on top, firing at random on civilians. These jeeps usually had four occupants: a driver, a gunner, and two observers. Over and over again, we would hear the sound of their machine guns as they drove around the city, aiming them at Jews. They were simply murdering people for the fun of it. On other occasions people were executed by the Nazis, on the spot, for some absurd "crime," such as walking on the sidewalk, instead of in the gutter, or having "unfavorable thoughts" about Germans. Day after day the "volkswagen" killings went on. People did everything they could to keep from walking in the streets. There was panic in Jewish homes, and no real way to fight back. Generally, the Germans driving the "volkswagens" were not Wehrmacht troops, but rather Gestapo or some special uniformed soldiers, the "SA," who were also called the "brown shirts."

Instinct was an important attribute in surviving the carnage. When people sensed that a "volkswagen" attack was about to take place, they would rush for the courtyards between buildings. There they could usually escape the machine gunnings. Every now and then, however, a "volkswagen" crew would turn their guns towards the courtyards. The resulting massacres were even bloodier than the main street killings, because the courtyards were filled with people trying to escape from the violence.

One day in November of 1939 I came home from working in the tailor shop to find my whole family weeping and sitting shiva—mourning for the dead. My parents told me that my sister Rachel had gone out that day and had not returned. There had been another attack on Jewish men. The Jews had piled the bodies of the dead on wagons and taken them to a mass grave for burial. It was then that my parents learned that Rachel was dead. She had been walking in the street when she was gunned down by the crew of a roving jeep. We were not allowed to bury her ourselves. The Germans had forbidden private funerals. She was buried in the mass grave with the other victims of the attack. On every street it was the same—families in mourning, families waiting for someone to come home. Every day there were arrests and killings. That was how we lived.

During this time the Germans were systematically withdrawing all Jewish rights. We were denied access to medications and hospitals. Epidemics of typhus and dysentery broke out, and many people died. Supplies of food and water were limited. While Catholics had adequate rations and privilege cards, which allowed them to buy most of the things that they wanted, Jewish families barely had enough for themselves, let alone the thousands of orphans that the Jewish community was now supporting. Jews were not allowed to travel from one city to another without special passes. We were barred from riding on streetcars or on trains, and couldn't even communicate with other communities or with relatives in other places.

Gradually, the identification rules for Jews became even more stringent. We were prohibited from going about our normal business in public. Then we were required to wear an armband with a Star of David on it, so that everyone could immediately identify us as Jews. We weren't even supposed to walk on the sidewalks. We were forced to walk in the gutters of the streets, wearing our arm-bands. Next, the synagogues were closed. We couldn't legally conduct morning Jewish worship with a minyan, which required ten men to be present. The penalty for any gathering of ten people or more in a room was death for everyone present. It was also illegal for more than three Jews to walk together in the street. Many families were forced to travel in separate groups of twos or threes to avoid being arrested.

# chapter 5

At this time my brother Maurice was a sheet-metal worker in a German-operated auto body repair shop in Warsaw. The Gestapo headquarters was housed nearby in a building that had formerly been the Polish Senate. The buildings had many rooms in the cellar where Polish officers and intellectuals were being held as hostages or prisoners. Some were Jews, though most were not. Many of the people being held had been brought in for interrogation and had never been released. One day Maurice was assigned to do some sheet-metal work in the Gestapo building. He told me that while he was working he could hear prisoners calling out names. Then prisoners in other cells would shout back the names of their hometowns. Maybe they wanted to find a neighbor who could tell their relatives of their fate.

Maurice also told me about the executions he had witnessed. These took place in a courtyard surrounded by beautiful flowers, trees, and shrubs. Before the killings the Germans would recite a list of "crimes" that each condemned man had allegedly committed. The charges invariably included some great plot to overthrow Hitler. They would also tell the Poles, "Today we are shooting you. Tomorrow we'll be shooting the French, and the day after, the English." As the Polish officers were about to die they told the Germans that Poland would "survive the terror and murder."

As time went on, we heard more tales of the screams and tortures that accompanied the interrogations. In February 1940, after registering for compulsory labor, as the Germans required, Maurice was taken away to Camp Karczow, about 30 kilometers from Warsaw, to dig trenches and build fortifications, such as heavy concrete bunkers. There he worked with hundreds of other Jewish men and boys. When he returned, he told us of the unbelievable cruelty he had witnessed at the camp.

Much of the abuse took place at night in the large barracks where all the inmates of the camp slept. Typically, the SS or SA members, who were in charge, would enter a barrack while the men were sleeping. They would turn on the lights and demand an immediate "inspection." This was not really an inspection but merely a euphemism the Germans used to justify their sadistic abuse of the inmates. For example, they might order a man to display some ability, to mimic an animal, by running, jumping, and scampering about on all fours. Frequently inmates who were unable to perform or whose performance did not impress their German masters properly, were murdered. Maurice said that as many as four or five murders would be committed during one inspection.

The inmates of the camp lived in constant fear. There was no safe time, day or night. Because of the "inspections" it was probably more dangerous during nonworking periods. Often the inmates were simply unable to meet the work demands placed on them by the Germans. Sickness, weakness, or any other reason for not obeying the German demands would result in torture and often death. Sometimes men were abused because some German decided the trenches were not deep enough.

The tortures took a variety of forms. An inmate who had been accused of being a slacker would have his hands tied to a bench. Then, the guards would beat him until he passed out. After that, the guards would splash water on his face to wake him. The beating and splashing were repeated several times until the victim was shot and thrown into a grave which he might have been forced to dig himself, before the torture began. At other times the guards would nail a man's hand to a table using a hammer and small nails. Then they would tell the victim that they were finished with him and that he was free to go. The poor man would struggle to get free, and the more he struggled, the greater his agony. There was no end to the malevolent creativity of these torturers. They would even tie a man's legs with a rope, then hang him upside down from the rafters. While he was struggling, they would then break his arms and legs with blows from hard sticks or clubs.

Fortunately, Maurice was a knowledgeable, competent worker. Also, one of the bosses liked him; in the labor camp it became his key to survival. He usually had enough to eat, and eventually he was released and allowed to return to

Warsaw. On the trip home he was recaptured for another labor camp project, but luckily he escaped.

By this time, my other brother, Nathan David, had been forced to work for a German SS outfit as a mechanic. He worked at various locations around Warsaw, on trucks, cars, and motorcycles. His job included one important benefit; he was given meat, beans, and bread, and whatever he did not eat on the job, he was able to bring home. Nathan David told me that the Germans in charge of the SS work units would whip the young men and women for no apparent reason. Before the war, some of the Germans had been thieves, criminals, and homosexuals, and, once the war began, torturing the Jews in their charge was some sort of game for them. They used many methods and would whip the workers sadistically.

Nathan David also told of other cruelties. The Germans would tie a handkerchief across the eyes of a Jewish worker. He would then be ordered to march in a certain direction, and inevitably would end up marching right into a wall. The German would then yell at him, "that's not the direction I ordered you to march in!" Then they would beat him and force him to run back and forth, while they sprayed him with a high-pressure water hose, knocking him to the ground. Another SS pastime was to tie a Jew to a horse's tail, and send him running in circles. This would cause the horse to start running, dragging the Jew behind. But the SS didn't need horses, fire hoses, or other props to play their continuing sadistic games on helpless victims. They would simply force a man to put his fingers on a door frame and then close the door on the fingers. While this was done, they would kick the man in the groin.

Nathan David eventually was able to find a different job with a unit of the Wehrmacht. He still performed some mechanic's work and other unskilled jobs, such as carrying things from one place to another, but the Wehrmacht members were not as brutal as the SS. Individual Wehrmacht soldiers would often not bother to torture Jews unless they were given a direct order to do so. There were exceptions, as always, to the rule. But, on the whole, my brother was able to work without the constant threat of beatings, torture, and death.

◆ ◆ ◆

The German dependence on forced manual labor was a very curious thing because, in fact, there was more torture and murder than work. They created labor forces which were organized into brigades. Men and women alike, from ages 15 to 65, were liable to be taken for the work brigades. Every day in February and March of 1940 these labor brigades could be seen marching off from Warsaw. There were few tools, and the work was very hard. Some people were forced to push railroad cars—cattle cars or coal cars. Those the Germans suspected of slacking off were whipped, but first, they were forced to remove their clothing so the whippings would be more effective. Women were often forced to remove their underwear and use the garments to wash the floors. Many of the workers never came back. Some were killed by the strain of the work, others died of the beatings; some were just shot.

◆ ◆ ◆

During this time, I continued to work in Bromberg's tailor shop. Most of my clients were Germans who worked for the occupation government. Some were gendarmes, and others members of the Gestapo. Some of them usually wore uniforms while others always wore civilian clothing. Most of these clients were cold and businesslike, but I did manage to have several informal conversations with a member of the Gestapo. This young man was about my age, perhaps twenty-five years old. He was a native Pole who had studied electrical engineering at the university. He spoke German fluently and worked for the Gestapo as an interpreter. I remember he was an officer, perhaps a junior lieutenant. He always ordered lots of clothes, both for himself and for his girlfriend.

One day in April 1940, when he was in the shop, he took me aside and said, "Carl, let me tell you something. I like you, and I want you to know that a ghetto is being built in Warsaw." He told me that all the Jews in Warsaw would have to live in the ghetto when it was completed. At the time, walls were under construction in many places, but it wasn't clear for what purpose. He told me that eventually the walls would enclose the ghetto, and that it was a secret from the general population. He advised me, for my own good, that it would be best for me to "get out of Warsaw because there will be many trials and tribulations, and some very hard times for Jews, and I do not want to think that you would be caught in the ghetto, for there will be no escape from it."

That night I went home and told my family what the officer had said. At that time my two brothers, Maurice and Nathan David, and my sister, Toba, were living with my parents. I repeated over and over the advice that the Gestapo officer had given me: "Get out before it's too late!" We had already lost Rachel; I hoped that we would find a way to leave Warsaw while keeping the rest of our family together.

Soon after my conversation with the officer the Nazis ordered all the Jews of Warsaw into the ghetto. The order was accompanied by a proviso that each person could take with him only one bundle of personal belongings. Everyone was encouraged to take their valuables.

I did not obey the order. I knew that, if I was to have any chance of surviving, I would have to get out of Warsaw. I decided to leave before the ghetto was completely enclosed. Getting out of the area presented another problem. Jews could not leave the city—whether by train, horse and buggy, or on foot. The ideal situation would have been to leave with my entire family. That was impossible. My parents were Orthodox Jews and would have been recognized as such as soon as they tried to leave the city. The punishment for a Jew trying to travel without authorization was death. My only chance was to dress as a Christian and to go alone. I could not risk my parents' or my brothers' and sister's lives by taking them along.

Saying goodbye was difficult. I had no idea if I would ever see my family again. The words did not come easily. But I told my parents I hoped to be successful in my journey and that later we might all be reunited. My father blessed my search for a new place to live, and told me that I was right to go, that this was for the best, and that, as soon as possible, we would be together again. In his eyes and in mine was the fear that this was the last time we would ever see each other.

# chapter 6

I was risking my life, both by leaving Warsaw and by pretending to be a Christian. I carried no documents, but I wore a crucifix around my neck. I hoped that such an obvious sign would discourage questions from the authorities. This deception, along with the fact that I was not wearing the required armband for Jews, would have meant death had I been caught. Nor did I have enough money to bribe my way out of any difficulty. I had only 200 zlotys, worth less than a dollar.

The Vistula River was my escape route from Warsaw. I bought a ticket for Kozienice and boarded ship. It was a commercial vessel normally used for transporting iron, coal, and lumber, and there were few comforts. I had no baggage, just the clothes on my back and the money.

On the ship I met a Jewish girl who had also slipped out of Warsaw. She suspected that I was a Jew and was running away. She asked me directly if I was a Jew, and I answered yes. We had a way to ask such things in Hebrew; the question was "Am-hu?" or "Are you one of our people?" We talked for a while and, after hearing about my plight, the girl invited me to go with her to her relatives' house in Kozienice. After traveling for a day and a night, the ship docked about 20 kilometers from Kozienice. There were lots of men, women, and children aboard, and many carried food. Apparently they were food dealers of some sort. But there were no Germans on board, and we had no problem debarking.

We walked toward Kozienice. We traveled at night to avoid detection by the Nazis. This was dangerous because it was impossible to know where the Germans might have erected checkpoints where we would have to produce identification papers. Finally, we arrived at her relatives' house. They fed me and let me spend the night in safety in their home. The next day, I thanked the girl and her family for their hospitality and said goodbye. One of my mother's sisters, my Aunt Toba, and her husband, my Uncle Mandel Friedman, lived in Radom, 20 kilometers away, and I wanted to be able to reach them. I was sure they would be able to help me get settled.

After I arrived in Radom I quickly found out that life there wasn't easy. Although Radom did not yet have a ghetto, the people were living under very strict rules. To go anywhere or do anything you needed a pass; to go to work, to ride on any form of transportation, even to go to a doctor or a clinic if you were sick.

I had hoped to stay with my Aunt Toba, a goodhearted and beautiful woman. When I arrived at her house, she tried to make me feel welcome, but it was obvious that she was under a terrible strain. The house in which she and her family lived consisted of a small kitchen and one large room. Their furniture had been stolen by Gentiles, yet they made a special place for me to sleep. To make matters worse, two of Toba's five children had been injured during German bombing raids and were dying. Two girls died from their wounds.

Food was in short supply, and we had to scrounge for it wherever we could. To make matters more difficult, the Germans had imposed strange regulations which made it dangerous to walk outside. For example, if you met a German on the street, you had to offer an appropriate greeting, such as, "Good morning." But the German might take offense at your courtesy and say something like, "Can't you see that I am a German and you are not my equal? How dare you speak to me?" It was a crime to anger a German, and they were ready to impose beatings at any time. "Crimes" could be invented on the spot, which meant that there was no sure way to avoid the beatings completely. As in Warsaw, the Christian residents of Radom fared much better than the Jews. They were seldom beaten for imaginary insults to the Germans.

Because of the conditions in Radom, I decided to move on. I set out to walk the fourteen kilometers to Wolanow. Again, I wore a cross and no armband. Fortunately, the rural stone and gravel road didn't have any German checkpoints. That's not to say that the road was unused. As I walked along, a Polish farmer, driving a horse-drawn wagon, passed by. I stopped him and asked if he would give me a ride to Wolanow. Before agreeing he wanted to know who I was. Anyone would have suspected that I was a Jew if I said my name was Rosenberg, so I told him that my name was Karl Rosalski. It was as dangerous to lie to the farmer as it was for him to give me a ride. Even though the farmers were relatively free to travel as they wished, the Germans could still stop a wagon and inspect its contents. I had no identification papers. There was no predicting what the Germans might say or do if we ran into them. We were lucky, however, and reached Wolanow without incident. The farmer drove straight towards Wolanow and dropped me off at the edge of the village. I asked him if I had to pay and he said no, he didn't want any money. It had taken less than an hour to get from Radom to Wolanow.

I found lodgings with another aunt, Rose Bojman, in Wolanow. After a day or two in town, I discovered that I needed a pass or, at the very least, some form of identification. Everyone had to have documents, and these were issued only by the Polish authorities. I made up my mind to go to the town hall and ask for a pass. I hoped that someone would take pity on me and do me a favor. After all, there were many refugees, and many of them didn't have adequate identification. When I reached the town hall I was surprised to discover that I recognized a young man who was working there. He was three or four years older than I, and I had gone to school with his brother. My parents and his parents had been good friends before the war, even though we were Jews and they were Christians. Here he was, a secretary in the office in which I was applying for a pass. This had to be a stroke of good luck.

"Hello!" I said. I saw that he recognized me, too. He asked me what I had come for. "Would you do me a favor?" I asked. "I need a pass. Can you help me get one?" As I was explaining my situation he suddenly got very angry. I couldn't understand why. Then he stood up and started insulting me, calling me a shameful, filthy Jew and many other insulting names. "What do you mean?" he screamed. "You're talking to me as if I was your friend. I'm not your servant! Get out now, or I'll turn you over to the authorities." It was then that I realized I had committed the sin of forgetting that times were different now. This was not before the war when Christians and Jews could, at least sometimes, relate to one another on a friendly basis. I had made the mistake of addressing my former acquaintance by his name.

I quickly apologized and backed out of his office, not even daring to turn around. My confidence was shattered. How was I going to get along? I had no documents and no way of getting any. This was an extremely dangerous moment in my life, one which I have never forgotten. Nor have I forgiven the man who threatened me with such danger.

Jews were arriving in Wolanow from many areas of Poland, adding as many as fifty to seventy-five people to a small town whose population had now grown to slightly above five hundred. These Jews were not coming to a place where they would be welcome or have even a minimum level of comfort. They had to find a place to stay, and they had to find work. Only after they were employed could they earn the right to remain in Wolanow. Refugees found themselves sleeping in sheds, in attics, and even in barns with cows and other animals, anywhere as long as they could get a roof over their heads.

Every once in a while, a refugee would enter town with a story that was a precursor of the horrors to come. I remember one Jew who walked into Wolanow with blood pouring from his arms, his legs, and his head, his clothes hanging in shreds. He had walked many miles from Lublin. In Yiddish he screamed, "The Germans are slaughtering us. They took the whole town, ordered them into cattle cars, and shipped them off to where I don't know, but to certain death." At the time, nobody believed him. They thought he was crazy. Then more and more refugees came into town, each with his own tale of horror.

One young man I befriended told me a particularly disturbing story that convinced me that the tales were true. He had come from a resort city thirty kilometers from Warsaw. It had a Jewish population of nearly twenty thousand when the town was taken over by a group called Reinhart's Commandos, a band of mercenaries authorized by the SS to manage the Jewish affairs of the city. Reinhart was probably an SS officer, perhaps with the high rank of Colonel. Most of his soldiers were Ukrainians. Reinhart's major purpose, it seemed, was to punish the people of the city and keep them contained for quick reassignment to work details. Loudspeakers were installed and were used to inform the captive Jewish population that they would be taken to work in nearby labor camps. The Nazis used those words countless times during the war. Sometimes they were true. Other times it was just a ploy to ensure cooperation. The people were told that they would be allowed to take along no more than one suitcase or one bundle of their personal belongings. All of their valuables such as jewelry, money, gold, or other items would have to be carried on their persons. They were also told that anyone found hiding in his home or anywhere else would be killed on the spot.

There was no escape from the city. The commandos had posted rings of guards at intervals around the city and at night illuminated the edges with huge spotlights. The Polish police, firemen, and other uniformed services were drafted to help keep the city surrounded. Finally the people were marched away. The children, the old, and the sick were marched off to an area where they were machine-gunned to death. The others were forced to march five kilometers to a train where they were then herded like cows into cattle cars totally unfit for human habitation and were constantly under the threat of torture and death at the least sign of resistance. Just before they were loaded onto the train, each person was given a piece of bread. This was not so much for nourishment as to give the Germans a means of counting how many bodies were being loaded in each train—to make the calculations all they had to do was to count the number of pieces of bread remaining.

The young man told me about the stench in the cattle cars, an odor caused by a six-inch layer of disinfectant powder that had the consistency of talc. The odor was almost unbearable due to its pungency. This man somehow managed to escape before he was taken away in the cattle car. What he told me brought about some very disturbing questions. Why were the Jews being singled out and treated this way? What had we done? What had we failed to do? I couldn't think of any answers that made sense.

There were also terrible stories about how Jews were being treated in Wolanow itself. The German authorities had been raiding this small town for a long time, banging on doors at night and taking the young people away to work. Usually those taken came back the next night, but some were never seen again. The Germans offered no explanations as to why these people never returned. Some may have been shot for not working hard enough; others for trying to escape, and a few may actually have escaped. The Jews who remained in Wolanow lived in constant fear, day and night. There was literally no place to hide and no way to escape.

Whenever the Germans needed a work party, they drove a convoy of trucks into town manned by soldiers with machine guns and rifles. Whoever they found, they would herd like cattle, prodding them with their guns. The raids usually took place after dark. To avoid getting caught, a group of us young men hid in the Catholic cemetery every night. The final resting place of the Polish Christians was one of the few places the Nazis never seemed to search. Some of those hiding in the cemetery lay in crypts where they managed to sleep. The rest of us, behind old tree stumps, were ready to scurry out into the night if it became necessary, but that never happened. When morning came, we would return home. The Polish Jews who lived in the area warned us that "the dead will haunt you for going into the cemetery." We didn't fear the dead. We were only afraid that the Germans would round us up, pack us into boxcars, and transport us to an unknown destination from which we would never return.

Meanwhile, the German military authorities began taking control of many acres of farmland surrounding Wolanow. There were lots of German Luftwaffe personnel in the area, and it soon became evident that they were going to build an air base, not to fly airplanes, but to train Luftwaffe personnel. Christian peasants were forcibly removed from their farms and evicted from their villages.

Eventually some thirty-five square kilometers were cleared. Christians who had lost their homes and farms were given aid in resettling and rebuilding their lives. Signs were erected asking for "volunteers" to work at the base. A Christian who "volunteered" would almost certainly get a job and suffer no ill effects. Jews could not expect such compassionate treatment.

In the meantime, it was harder than ever to find food, and to do this, we were forced to take strange measures. Because the supply of food was controlled by the Nazis, the Jews had to sneak out at night to the farmers' fields to buy or trade for supplies. It was one thing to purchase potatoes or onions, but meat was a problem; most Jews would eat only kosher meat, and the farmers, who were not Jews, did not slaughter their cows in the ritual manner. The only thing to do was to buy a cow, and slaughter it ourselves. But how would we hide so large an animal as a cow? My uncles, who were butchers, concocted a scheme. We bought a young bull and walked it back to the village late at night. Then we made a ladder with rungs leading up to the attic, and somehow, after much pushing and shoving, got the bull upstairs. Then we summoned a *shochet,* a ritual slaughterer. He slaughtered the cow in accordance with kosher law. My uncles then took over. Even the hide was put to good use. It was given to the local Christian shoemaker.

Life grew more dangerous for us as the air base neared completion. Reports of Jews being arrested on the roads between villages were often followed by reports of killings. We would hear stories from refugees who saw dead bodies lying on the sides of the roads. The Germans had set traps at the crossroads. Jews, aware of this, often had to detour for a kilometer or two into fields or orchards, moving through the bushes on all fours at times, making sure not to utter a sound.

The Germans would explain that the killings were part of an "anti-smuggling" campaign, but in many cases the murdered Jews were carrying only a little food and nothing else.

# chapter 7

**B**y May of 1940, the uncertainty of such an existence led me to take a desperate gamble. I decided to go to the base and volunteer my services. In that way I might be able to get papers and avoid being arrested and transported in the cattle cars or simply killed for some crazy violation like thinking "bad thoughts" about the Germans.

The base was about two and a half kilometers from Wolanow. I walked up to the gate and told the guard that I was responding to the signs and that I wanted to volunteer for work. I also made sure that he understood that I was a tailor. He didn't seem too impressed. He did want to know details about my religion. I told him that I was Jewish and that I was a native Pole. The guard picked up the telephone and called the main office. He told the superintendent that a Jewish tailor was volunteering his services. Then he escorted me directly to the superintendent's office.

The superintendent immediately dismissed the guard. Then he closed the door and asked me some questions. After I told him a bit about myself, he locked the door and pulled down the window shades. I began to worry. Why was he acting so strangely? He then asked me to "take a chair." That was even stranger. Germans in positions of authority would never ask a Jew to sit in their offices. "Don't be afraid of me," he said quietly. "I am a German, but I am not a Nazi. In my heart and soul, I am a Christian."

This man's name was Otto Busse, a civil engineer, charged with the construction at Wolanow of the Luftwaffe #2 training base for pilots and airmen. Naturally, I found it difficult to believe what Busse said. He seemed so completely different from all the other Germans I had ever met.

I asked him if he was going to employ me. He smiled and said, "Yes." Then he picked up a pen and wrote instructions to have a pass and identification documents issued to me. I was to be his personal tailor and the identification contained a proviso that I could not be taken on any work projects without his specific permission. Before dismissing me Busse said, "Be here tomorrow so we can set you up to be my tailor."

The happiness I felt is difficult to explain. Busse was a powerful, impressive, and kind man who had many people working for him. The risk he took in hiring me was just as great as the one I took in looking for work at the base.

Busse set me up in a small shop in Wolanow. A sign was placed in the window stating that I was working under the direct orders of the base commander. I made suits from materials he supplied. He provided me with documents that allowed me to carry clothing to and from the base without hindrance. I also received a small salary which I spent on food. Often the feelings of good fortune and an almost satisfied stomach were simply overwhelming. I was doing very well, considering the circumstances at the time. The base had some 10,000 workers from all the occupied countries. I noticed that a handful of them were Jews from Germany. They apparently were key administrative personnel and received protection from the firms they worked for, firms that were contractors at the base.

I told some other young Jews in Wolanow about my good luck in getting the job and urged them to also seek work at the base. They were understandably skeptical, but Busse usually hired those who dared to ask for work. As a result of his help some 200 Jews got jobs at the base. Some were carpenters, plumbers, electricians, and laborers. Others, who were educated and were fluent in German, got jobs as office workers on the base. All this took place in the spring and early summer of 1940.

◆◆◆

I had not forgotten my parents who were still in the Warsaw ghetto. The ghetto was still open, but it was apparent that it would soon be closed off from the outside world. The Jews would be kept inside, and entry and exit would be forbidden.

I learned that my brother, Maurice, had been captured on the streets of Warsaw and sent to help build the German defense lines between the Russian and German armies. He had been taken to the lines near Lublin. The Germans were having trenches dug as preparation for war with Russia, even though, as a result of the Hitler-Stalin pact, Germany was at peace with Russia. After a few months, Maurice was allowed to return to Warsaw. To avoid being captured again by the Germans, he and my younger brother, Nathan David, posed as Christians and slipped away from Warsaw. They traveled by train and managed to reach Wolanow safely. My parents and my sister, Toba, remained in Warsaw.

My brothers, like me, spoke German well, and it was a relatively simple matter to find them jobs at the base. Nathan David became a telephone switchboard operator at the central building. Maurice got a job at the electrical parts issue center. He was responsible for inventory control and keeping records of all parts issued. Although neither of my brothers received much money for their work, they did get reasonable amounts of bread, margarine, and other food. But the most important benefit was the identity passes that shielded them from at least some of the daily risks we faced as Jews in Nazi-controlled Poland.

Each of us got to know some of the German workers at the base. Maurice made the acquaintance of a truck driver who was ferrying building materials in and out of Warsaw. One day, Maurice asked if he could accompany this man into the ghetto, posing as a laborer. He told him he wanted to rescue our parents and Toba before the ghetto was completely closed off. We all realized that it was only a matter of time before everyone in the ghetto would be killed. The driver agreed, and Busse helped by providing the necessary passes and papers.

Once they reached Warsaw, Maurice and the driver had my parents and Toba lie in the bed of the truck and covered them with construction materials. Then they just drove out of the ghetto. Busse had given the driver papers stating that the truck carried materials urgently needed at the base, and that the cargo need not be checked, so no one stopped them.

Once again, our entire family was living in Wolanow. We rented a one-room house, and all six of us lived there. The room contained a kitchen with an oven, and there was an outhouse. Busse himself hired Toba as a seamstress and personal cook and laundry helper for his family. She worked at their house on the air base grounds. After a while, we moved to another house in the Jewish section of Wolanow.

During this time many people were being jailed, beaten, abused, and shot. We were protected by Otto Busse, and our family avoided serious harm. Maurice was arrested once, when he found a shirt lying in the mud and took it home. He washed the shirt and was wearing it when its owner accused him of having stolen it. Apparently, the shirt had been blown off a clothesline and had landed in the mud. Busse intervened and saved him from a possible death sentence. Jews were being murdered every day for such trivial offenses.

The kindness of Otto Busse and his wife is difficult to describe. They were in their early thirties with a five-year-old son. They took great interest in their appearances, and often, after I had completed a particular garment, Mrs. Busse would give me bread, sugar, and flour, which she said were "for your mother." She always said, "Let your mother bake for you."

◆ ◆ ◆

By this time the Germans had already begun to systematically starve the Jews in occupied Poland. This was easily accomplished through cutting Jewish food rations. The emergency supplies of flour and potatoes stored by each family were soon exhausted. A small number of Jews were successful farmers, but the Germans confiscated all their livestock using "the laws of occupation" as their excuse. Under these restrictive laws, no Jew was allowed to own animals. These "laws" were also used to justify raiding cellars of Jewish houses and farms to seize food supplies beyond the immediate needs of the day. Gendarmes, two or three at a time, would enter houses unannounced and begin checking the cooking pots. If they found meat, they would ask lots of questions about its source and how it had been purchased. Fortunately, however, the police maintained a somewhat predictable inspection schedule. So most people cooked only very late at night. Still, doing so was dangerous at any time of day. Even the delightful aroma of fresh baked bread could trigger an impromptu inspection because that also was forbidden.

The changes in our daily lives were subtle at first. Then they began to take on the quality of a nightmare. In the Radom-Wolanow area, shopkeepers were arrested, first a butcher, then several dry-goods merchants. To the best of my knowledge all were shot. Then one day the post office stopped delivering mail from Jews in other cities. Now we were completely cut off from relatives and friends who didn't live in the immediate vicinity.

One night several Jews were arrested near Wolanow. Two were butchers, one of whom had been traveling without a pass. They were taken to the police station in town where the Germans beat and tortured them, breaking their ribs and damaging their kidneys. In the morning, the Germans shot them. They ordered some Polish Christians to load the corpses onto a small horse-drawn wagon, which was crudely thrown together and consisted merely of a bottom board and two side boards. The horse pulled the driverless wagon around town so that everyone could see the bodies. A large placard, attached to the wagon, instructed the Jewish population to bury the bodies immediately.

As a warning to the Polish Christians who might want to help Jews, the Germans selected eight of them at random from different parts of town and shot them on the spot. Then they ordered the local Christians to bury the bodies and warned them that if they dealt with Jews in any way they, too, would face a firing squad.

One day in the spring of 1941, a sanitation inspector, escorted by several Polish police armed with rifles, made a tour of Wolanow. During the tour, he discovered that the Jewish part of town didn't have a proper sewage system. Each home had a small barrel for waste and no running water. Inhabitants fetched water from a well in the center of town and dumped their sewage into a pool just outside of town. It was quite deep and very dirty. When the inspector discovered the pool, he demanded to know who was responsible for the open-air cesspool. He was told that it was the waste of the Jews, so he ordered the police to round up all the Jews they could find. Fifty men and women were gathered and ordered to walk fully clothed into the cesspool. The water rose over the heads of many, and the panic was terrible. When they were finally allowed to emerge, the stink and filth were beyond belief. I remember the smell, the matted wet hair, and the terror on the faces of my poor fellow Jews. After the pool had been vacated, the inspector ordered the Jews to get shovels and fill the pool with dirt. My sister Toba was one of those forced to submerge in the cesspool.

Finally, on June 22, 1941, the provincial governor in Radom ordered all Jews confined into ghettos. Since we were already in the equivalent of one, the order was absurd. As it was, no one was allowed to take even one step out onto the fields at the edge of town without the threat of being killed. The German in charge of the relocation told the leaders of the Jewish community in Wolanow that if the Jews could come up with one and a half kilos of gold, he would cancel the order. Requests were made to all the families, and the gold was collected and given to the German official. He took the money but did not cancel the order as he had promised. Those Jews not living in the Jewish section, now defined as the ghetto, were required to pack their things, and relocate into the now crowded Jewish part of town. As it turned out, the house we had moved to several months ago was in this section. We had escaped from one ghetto only to move into another.

## chapter 8

At the end of May 1942 I happened to see a German newspaper, the *Volkische Beobachter* and read an article by Alred Rosenberg entitled, "The Jewish Question Is Finished." I read it twice and wondered what it all meant. I talked with the other Jewish leaders in Wolanow, and we decided that the article probably meant that the Jews were going to be killed en masse by the Germans. What else could the most vitriolic anti-Semite in German government mean by the "Jewish Question" being "finished"? We expected that in a short time all the Jews in the ghettos would be evacuated to areas where they would be killed. Our only hope was to become indispensable to the Germans in some way so that they wouldn't be too eager to have us murdered. With the help of Busse we already had some five hundred Jews working at the air base, but there were many more living in the ghetto who didn't work at the base. These Jews would surely be doomed when the Germans decided to transport them to their "final solution."

After some discussion, our "committee" agreed on a plan. There was an old labor camp adjacent to the air base that had been occupied until recently by Russian prisoners of war. It had been abandoned. Maybe all the Jews from the ghetto could be moved into the camp as "laborers" and the Germans would let us alone, particularly if it seemed that we were needed for their war effort. It was a shot in the dark, but since we hadn't come up with anything better, we decided to try to make it happen. Since, of all the members of our committee, I was closest to Busse, it was decided that I should talk with him and try to convince him to have us moved to the Russian camp. Time was of the essence, so I immediately went to the base and found Busse in his office.

"What brings you here, Carl?" he asked.

"Did you read the article in the *Volkische Beobachter* about the 'Jewish Question?'"

Just as he did that first time he met me, Busse closed the door. "What do you have in mind?" he asked.

"You have a former Russian POW camp over there that could be used to save us." I said. "You could call it a 'concentration camp' and concentrate over a thousand Jews there and we would be saved."

"But how could I do that?"

I told him that he could argue that he needed more laborers to finish construction on the base and that he needed the camp to house the Jewish workers.

"But I couldn't say the camp was for 'Jews.' It would never be approved. Better, I'll say it's for Polish workers." So Busse wrote a letter requesting approval for the conversion of the POW camp and in a week he called me in and showed me a document authorizing him to create a concentration camp for a thousand workers. I was so happy. I knew that now we would at least have a chance to stay alive.

Busse and I went over to the camp to see what needed to be done to get it ready for our community. We found it in terrible condition.

"Mr. Busse," I said, "let's get organized and get the camp cleaned up and painted right away." This was important as it was filthy and not fit to live in, and we were worried that if we didn't act quickly the Germans might begin evacuating the ghetto and send us to our deaths. So we got painters and carpenters and rehabilitated the camp.

Before we started painting, though, I noticed some strange scribblings on the walls of the barracks. They were messages, many written in blood by the Russian prisoners. These soldiers wanted to let the world know that they had been there. They wrote their names, along with their dates of birth, and their military ranks. The Russians had all died, either from overwork, beatings, or diseases like typhus. As we painted over the walls, obliterating their scribblings, all records of their presence there vanished forever.

The camp was ready just in time, because the Germans had already been organizing the evacuation of the ghetto. By then, we had several thousand Jews crammed into it. They had come from all over the area, even from Radom. Busse had been authorized to have only one thousand workers in the camp. We were able to persuade him to take on fifteen hundred, but that was his limit. I knew that the remaining Jews, those who didn't have work permits for the base, would be taken away and killed, but there was nothing more that I or anyone else could do. Just before the evacuation, several of the Jews who were not going to the camp thanked us for our efforts. They knew that we had tried to have them all placed in the camp. They also realized that their chances of survival were virtually zero once they were taken away from the Wolanow ghetto. I remember one woman, Hanna, who was an invalid. Just before she was evacuated, I went to her house to say goodbye to her. She was so happy that I came, and I remember her words so well: "Carl, so help me God, you will be the one to survive this tragedy. I can see how much good you've done for us." Shortly afterwards she was taken out of her house and placed on a horse-drawn wagon on some straw to be evacuated to Szydlowiedz along with the others. I later heard that she died a few hours later while still on the wagon. Those who survived the trip were kept at Szydlowiedz for a few days, until they were loaded onto cattle cars, which, I later found out, took them to Treblinka.

No provisions had been made for moving our possessions into the POW camp, and had it not been for the generosity of Busse we wouldn't have been able to take even a small amount of utensils, furniture, and home furnishings to the camp. Busse volunteered some heavy transport trucks from the base and several squads of airmen to help move the Jewish people and their possessions from the ghetto to the camp. He even came over himself to supervise the operation.

Had we not been able to take these possessions, few of us would have survived the winter, which was very cold, even for Poland. The snow was at least knee-deep a good part of the time, and temperatures often went down to close to zero. The camp was encircled by heavy barbed-wire fences. The living conditions were wretched. Only a few of us had winter clothing, and many didn't even have shoes. About 200 men and women were sick, but there was no clinic or infirmary to go to.

Once we arrived at the camp, Busse had all of us assemble and made a short speech. He told us that no one should ever utter even a single word of complaint to any of the Germans at the base. Otherwise he would be placed in danger for what he had done and he would no longer be able to protect us. Then he left to let us organize.

The day after the eviction of all the Jews from Wolanow, I asked Busse if I could go back to the ghetto to see what it was like, now that all had left. He looked at me as if I was crazy. "You can't go there," he told me. "You'll be shot!"

"I don't mean to go alone," I said. "Get me a soldier and a horse-drawn carriage, and issue some orders that I'm to get some tailoring supplies from town."

Somehow, my argument convinced him, and he made all the arrangements. When I arrived in the ghetto, I was amazed. The streets were totally deserted and I couldn't hear a sound. I went to my own house and tried to find a suit that my sister Toby, in her rush to leave, had inadvertently left in the house. I noticed that nothing had been touched. The Polish Christians had kept out of the ghetto. After I left the house and was getting into the carriage, a young Pole who was walking in the street noticed me. He came over, looking surprised. "Did you come back? I thought you had all left."

"I'm just in town looking for tailoring supplies," I said.

Then he told me a story. "You know the man who lived in the house over there, next to the synagogue?" The man who had lived there was a landowner who also owned a flour mill. Every year he would donate potatoes to plant, food, and other things to the poor Christian farmers and their families. "This man," the Pole said, "refused to be evacuated. His wife and his children left with the other Jews, but he stayed. After all the Jews had gone, the gendarmes went through the ghetto to be sure that no one was there and found him sitting at his desk studying Hebrew scriptures. A German came over to him and shouted: 'What are you doing here?' The man replied, 'This is my home, this is my land, and if you are going to kill me, I'd rather you shoot me here, than I should have to see my people die.' The German took out his gun and shot him, then ordered the local Poles to take him out and bury him."

The following day Busse contacted the various Germans in charge of different departments on the base and told them about the new pool of laborers that had just arrived, many of whom were skilled. The Germans were happy to have us working for them, and those Jews who hadn't already been working at the base were quickly assigned to jobs. The first few months at the camp were very difficult, mostly because of a shortage of food. The SS were supposed to have provided sustenance for the inmates, but for some reason the paperwork was still pending and no food had arrived. Busse kept issuing memos to the SS, but it took three months for the supplies to start being trucked in. In the meantime, Busse secretly gave us small shipments of food from the base, and we got more from local farmers by bartering clothing, jewelry, and any other possessions we might have had.

# chapter 9

In the Wolanow camp most of us were required to appear at six in the morning to be assigned to work details. Generally, my mother worked in the camp kitchen, my father as a janitor at the base, and my sister Toba worked for the Busse family. My brothers and I, however, continued on special assignment at the air base. As a result, we had special passes which kept us from being herded into the workforces.

But the passes did not protect us from abuse, so I had to be careful to avoid trouble. For example, I never traveled anywhere alone. People alone were targets for the Polish camp police who were Christian Poles and who took their assignments as "police" very seriously. The Nazis had given them black uniforms and weapons. We called them the "black traitors," and they seemed to be everywhere, intimidating and beating us and causing trouble. They had the authority to force us to do whatever they wished. There were also the Jewish camp police, who were supposed to keep order but who had little authority and, of course, were never given weapons.

The "black traitors" were especially cruel in the mornings. They would make sweeps through the camp looking for anyone they thought was trying to avoid the work details. At that time, all able-bodied men were required to show up for work details, unless they had special passes like my brothers' and mine. Sometimes those who were sick or shoeless hid out in the barracks. This turned out to be more dangerous than reporting for work, even under freezing conditions. A vile German named Barkmann would start searching the camp for "slackers." Barkmann was responsible for all the labor assignments in the camp. Fifteen minutes after the first work detail departed he began his search. He was assisted by another man named Joseph Bannah who always carried a whip and a rifle and who enjoyed whipping women inmates as they headed towards their work assignments.

During one of the inspections, Barkmann found sixteen people hiding. He ordered the sixteen to line up in the camp yard. One of these was my fourteen-year-old cousin, Bluma Bojman. Bluma was the only female in the group. None were dressed for the cold; in fact, several had no shoes, and Bluma had only a rag for a coat. Barkmann ordered all sixteen locked up in the solitary confinement shack that had been known as the "death house" during the days of the Russian POWs. The shack was made of heavy barbed wire stretched between poles with straw thatched between the wires. It had a heavy, reinforced door which was secured with a strong lock. There was no furniture, merely the bare ground on which the prisoners could sit or stand. There was no way it could be considered a shelter. It was just a place to store people until they were killed.

When Bluma was taken to the "death house," I was suffering from typhus, a disease which was often fatal for inmates in the camp, and I was confined to bed. Normally, anyone who contracted this dread disease was killed. Barkmann would order one of the camp doctors to inject the sick person with arsenic. But he needed to keep me around because I made his suits in my tailor shop. So instead of condemning me to death, he covered up the fact that I had typhus by referring to my illness as a cold and influenza. He even gave me some medicine to help me recover, although there really wasn't any cure except the willpower to survive. I still remember the sickness. I felt as if I was flying or floating as I lay delirious with fever—it was like a nightmare.

Barkmann had added some more privileges to those we had already received from Otto Busse, and our family was allowed to live in a farmhouse on the camp grounds. For some unknown reason the house had not been destroyed when the prisoner of war camp was built. It even had an oven for baking bread. From the window, my mother had witnessed the roundup that netted Bluma and had seen the entire group locked up in the "death house." The Jewish camp police captain took the key and returned to the Jewish police headquarters.

My mother came to tell me what had happened, crying hysterically, and said to me in Yiddish, using my name, as she frequently did, when she spoke with me affection. "Please get up if you can, Kiwa. They are going to shoot her. Maybe you can save her." Even though no one survived the "death house," and though

I was in bed with a high fever with my senses foggy, I decided to try to save Bluma. For a while, I would be drifting, and then after a few minutes I seemed to wake up again and asked my mother what had happened? She told me once more about Bluma and the others who had been taken to the "death house."

I don't know where I got the strength to get out of bed. Normally, anyone recovering from typhus would have needed help just to walk, because the prolonged fever would have sapped his natural strength. Nevertheless, I woke up very quickly, as though nothing had been bothering me even though I had been near death for ten days. I asked my mother to get my boots. I also had a warm coat which I put on. While I was dressing, my mother protested. "How are you going to make it through the snow? It's up to your knees, at least."

I ignored her questions, went out the door and over to a sentry who was standing near the "death house" and asked, "Where is the key?" He replied, "Hey, are you crazy?" I repeated my question as forcefully as I could. "Tell me who has the key," I demanded. The sentry raised his voice and tried to match my tone. "He's crazy," he said, but then he told me that Emerglik, the police captain, had it.

I went straight to the police station, and told the first policeman I saw that I wanted to see Emerglik right away. I probably raised my voice a little when I demanded to see him. The policeman pointed to Emerglik's private office and said, "He's in there." Emerglik had originally been appointed by Otto Busse as chief of the Jewish camp police. The other Jewish camp policemen worked under Emerglik and were responsible to him.

I stormed into his office. "You know I've been sick with typhus," I told him, "but now I am up and in full possession of my faculties. I know you have a girl named Bluma Bojman locked up. She is my cousin. I want her out—out of that house," I said. Emerglik was stunned. The camp police weren't used to having inmates tell them who they could lock up and who they had to release. He reacted the same as the guards, saying loudly in Polish that I was crazy. "Come, take him away," he ordered. "He's lost his mind and doesn't know what he's talking about."

The camp police tried to pull me from Emerglik's office, but I resisted. "Don't touch me," I said. "If you do you will be sorry. All of you. You know who I am." Then turning again to Emerglik I said, "Now Emerglik, I want the key." He said he was afraid the whole group would escape. I reassured him, saying, "If anything happens, just tell whoever asks that I forced you to give me the key." And I added, "If anything does happen, it will be my responsibility. I will be shot, not you." Emerglik just looked at me and said again, "He is crazy." I became very angry. I looked closely at each man in the room and said, "Look. It will be your life, my life, and her life. All of you who try to stop me will be dead tomorrow."

It apparently began to dawn on Emerglik that I was in control of myself. I said, "You know I can do it." He thought for a moment and then relented. He handed me the key and ordered four policemen to accompany me back to the "death house." As we left the police building, I could hear the policemen asking each other, "How in hell can he walk in the snow?" They all agreed that I was indeed mad.

Ironically, one of the camp police who was assigned to go with me was my old school friend, Mier Patron, who had grown up next door to Bluma. "Mier," I said. "Are you on my side? I want you to be with me. We have to get Bluma out."

None of us really had any idea as to how we rescue Bluma. The fifteen young men inside the "death house" would certainly try to escape the minute we tried to get Bluma out of the shack. Also, the situation was urgent. We had to rescue Bluma before the Ukrainian death squad arrived to kill everyone inside. These Ukrainians were mercenaries who worked for the Germans as executioners. The Germans would telephone, and the Ukrainians would report to whatever camp held Jews that the Germans wanted killed. We knew that the Ukrainians had been called more than ninety minutes earlier, and that they would arrive at any minute, now. Time was growing short.

Emerglik followed us out. I told him that he had saved his own life by helping me but that now he could do no more. "Stay put," I told him. "The Ukrainians will want to know why there aren't sixteen as they were told," he said. But the point of no return had already been reached. Whatever the consequences, we were on our way to rescue Bluma. I left him standing there in the cold.

It was freezing. The prisoners in that house of death were shivering from the cold. Bluma was hysterical when I called to her as we neared that terrible place. "Bluma, come to the door. I want to talk with you."

The men inside were suspicious, but they allowed her to come to the door. "Please come closer," I pleaded, and the men obliged by pushing her. As she got close enough for me to whisper, I told her that I had a key and that we were going to try and get her out. "Just stand next to the door," I urged.

I had no strength left after the fever had subsided, and the four others braced themselves and pushed the door open so there was just a crack. I pulled on Bluma as they pushed, and she slipped out. The men inside fought hard to escape. They knew they were facing death very soon. They shouted, "Save me, get me out of here." Their cries became a roar. It wrenched our hearts to leave them there, but we knew that if they all escaped, many more would die.

Somehow we managed to lock the door again. I gave the key to one of the camp policemen to return to Emerglik's office, and I took Bluma to our house.

We put her to bed and gave her something warm to drink. My mother cried for a long time, even though Bluma was safe, back in the house. We all sat around waiting for her to recover and to learn what would happen when the Ukrainians arrived.

About half an hour later an SS truck bringing them arrived at the "death house." They waited until Barkmann showed up in the three-wheeled vehicle he always used. Barkmann ordered the door opened. As the prisoners emerged from the shack, some of them began to run. The six Ukrainians raised their rifles and mowed down all of the prisoners.

A few of them tried to hide inside by pulling themselves up into the rafters. After the Ukrainians shot the men who had been hiding in the shack, Barkmann went inside to see if anyone was left. He must have found some, because we could hear the sound of shooting from inside. Suddenly one man burst out, running toward a nearby field. As he did so, Barkmann raised his rifle and shot him. He was hit in the leg and fell to the ground. Barkmann ordered some of the inmates to drag him over to an open grave. Then Barkmann shot the man.

The camp police picked up the rest of the bodies and dropped them into the same common grave. One was always ready. When it was filled, another was dug immediately. The fifteen bodies filled the waiting grave, and the camp police dug another that would be available for the next group of corpses. Apparently, they never noticed that one "body" was missing.

My mother was overcome with joy. Her tears of relief eventually gave way to prayers, thanking God that I had had the courage and the strength to rescue Bluma. It was amazing, considering that I was still recovering from typhus. I think the courage came from seeing my mother crying so as she woke me from my feverish delirium. The next morning I was back at work in the tailor shop.

The men in the "death house" had faced impossible odds and died courageously trying to escape. Bluma survived the war and settled in Omaha, Nebraska.

## chapter 10

In November of 1942 Busse received orders to leave the air base. His superiors had accused him of being a "Jew lover," and, as punishment, had transferred him to the Russian front. Before Busse left he called me into his office, and told me the news. I was shocked to learn of his transfer and feared for the safety of our Jewish community. Busse shook my hand and said, "I wish you and your family luck in surviving the war." Then he drove over to the camp and talked to my mother. He told her, "Mother Rosenberg, I'm leaving, but I will do all I can to see that you are protected after I leave." Mother cried as he left.

The next day Busse called me into his office to introduce me to his replacement, Herman Rubbi. "Herman," he said, "I would like you to meet the Schneidermeister who has worked here since 1940. I want you to know he deserves good treatment. He is honest and devoted to the base and to our people. Take good care of him." Then Busse left with his wife and his son.

Rubbi told me that I would continue to work in my tailor shop. I would be responsible for his tailoring as I was for Busse, but the intimacy I shared with Busse was gone. Rubbi was from Stuttgart, and I had heard that he had been a member of the Hitler Youth. Still, I hoped that even if he wasn't helpful or friendly to us Jews, as Busse had been, at least he might leave us alone.

◆ ◆ ◆

One beautiful sunny day in the fall of 1942, shortly after Busse was sent to the

Russian front, four Gestapo men drove into the camp. They had heard rumors that there were Jewish children there who were too young to have work permits and, consequently, weren't supposed to live in the camp. Perhaps, the same informants who turned in Busse as a "Jew lover" had also informed the Gestapo about the children.

Emerglik, the Jewish camp police captain, was ordered to conduct an inspection, but, being Jewish, he did not look too hard and didn't find any of the children. So the Gestapo did their own inspection and found 18 children who were between one and ten years old. Fortunately, not all the children were found. Many, particularly the older ones, found good hiding places. One of my cousins hid under a big pile of leaves. Another, in a barrel. But for the families of the 18 the day was tragic.

The Gestapo man in charge ordered all the mothers of the 18 children to assemble with their children and he addressed them. "Mothers," he said, "we want you to live, to continue to work for the Reich, but your children have no right to be here because they don't produce. So we want to take the children away." The mothers began to cry and begged to be allowed to keep their children. But the man said: "Either you live and work without your children or we will take you along with the children." Everyone knew that that meant death. But all the mothers, without exception, decided to remain with their children. Once the inevitability of their fate became clear, the crying and lamenting stopped. One mother shouted: "If you want to kill our children you'll have to kill us too. We won't produce anything for the Third Reich if you take our children from us." Another yelled, "We are Jewish mothers. We won't sacrifice our children for our lives. We are strong, we have the strength of lionesses to lay down our lives."

A truck drove up and the women were ordered to climb aboard, carrying their children. How proud they looked as they climbed aboard that truck! Then they were driven away. We later learned from a Polish farmer that the mothers and their children had been taken to a ravine in the woods, about fifteen kilometers away, where they were all shot. The Gestapo then ordered some Polish farmers in the area to bury them.

◆ ◆ ◆

One day, about a week after Busse left, I was working in my tailor shop on the base when some Christian Poles who worked in the shop told me they had heard that all the Jews were being massacred in the Wolanow camp. I left the shop and raced back to the camp. As I entered, I saw over one hundred and thirty of my Jewish campmates lying on the ground, covered with blood. It looked like a battlefield. Some other inmates were standing nearby, dazed, and I asked what had happened. They told me that after work that day, Rubbi had ordered one hundred and thirty-five men and women who worked at the base to assemble, some children as young as twelve. Rubbi announced that they were no longer needed to work at the base. Then he ordered them to march to the camp. A truckload of a dozen Ukrainians was waiting. Rubbi arrived and told Barkmann and Bannah to bring some buckets. He ordered the inmates to throw all their rings, earrings, and other jewelry into the buckets. Some of the survivors said they could hear the Germans debating among themselves as to whether to have the inmates shot with their clothes on, or to have them strip and then kill them naked. They decided to leave them dressed. Then the Ukrainians shot the prisoners in a barrage of rifle fire.

I found my mother in tears. She told me that just before the massacre, Rubbi had gone searching around the base looking for some of the Jews who were not needed for work and who might be hiding, particularly in the storage bins for the coal used to heat the barracks. He found my uncle, my mother's brother, Aba Bojman, along with another man. Rubbi then personally drove the two men to the camp and turned them over to the Ukrainians who immediately shot them. My mother also told me that she had been hiding two young men in our house at the camp, a cousin of mine who was fourteen and another boy who was only twelve, the son of her oldest brother. Rubbi, continuing his search for Jews who weren't authorized to work at the base, had entered our house, and had found them hiding under a bed. He dragged them out and took these two young men to the Ukrainians and they were also shot.

After the shooting Rubbi got in his car and left, not before he gave Barkmann and Bannah orders to have all the clothing removed from the victims' bodies and to be sure that nothing of value was left on them. Although there was always an open grave in the camp ready for any dead inmates, it was too small to hold all the victims of this massacre. The Jewish camp police, along with some other Jewish men who remained, were ordered to dig a new, large open grave, to remove the clothes from the victims, and then to throw the dead into the grave.

Barkmann and Rubbi left before the dead had been searched, but Bannah remained to supervise the search and the burial. Bannah was then supposed to deliver all the valuables directly to Rubbi's office. Some of the camp police, however, noticed that Bannah was taking some of the valuables that had been collected and putting them in his own pockets.

Afterwards the clothes of the dead were brought over to the Jewish Police headquarters to be distributed to those of us who were still alive. We had not been given any new clothes since we had arrived at the camp, and the clothes of the dead, even worn and full of holes and patches, might save some of our lives during the cold winter that lay ahead.

As the Jewish camp police were removing the clothes from the victims, one of them heard a voice whispering, "Listen, I am alive. . . . I am just acting dead, but I'm shot in the leg." The policeman quietly told the others what he had heard. They pretended the man was dead and acted as if they were going to bury him. When Bannah left, they took him to a men's barrack where a Jewish camp doctor treated his leg and kept him there. All the others were buried.

The next day Barkmann and Bannah conducted an inspection of the barracks and found this man. There hadn't been anyplace to hide him. Barkmann and Bannah asked the doctor what had happened to this man who was obviously wounded. Bannah wanted to know if he had survived the shooting the day before. The doctor had to tell them that he had indeed survived but he also said that he was strong and healthy, and that after his leg healed he would be able to do useful work for the Germans.

When the doctor explained that the man would recover, Barkmann said, "Are you trying to tell me that this man is going to be able to work?" Then he took out a bottle of arsenic and ordered Przyticky to inject the poor man with the poison. Przyticky had no choice but to comply, otherwise he would have been shot on the spot. After the doctor had administered the injection, the man began to writhe in agony, screaming in pain. He said in Yiddish, "I'm dying, but you people . . . remember the Germans and revenge death for death." Then he breathed his last.

The new commander, Rubbi, possessed none of Busse's generosity or compassion. Instead, as a former member of the Hitler Youth organization, he had as much hatred for Jews as the most rabid of the Nazis. He was also sadistic and would not hesitate to murder a Jew for as trivial a reason as not liking the poor victim's face. He would say something like, "You don't belong to the human race," and then have him killed. Sometimes he would do it himself. At other times he ordered a subordinate to perform the dirty work. I remember once when he shot a good worker named Leibisch Ackerman. Rubbi marched him to the edge of an open grave and shot him with his pistol. He also murdered a boy of fourteen because he was caught with a dead chicken in his rucksack.

## chapter 11

As long as Busse had been in charge of the camp, Bannah had no power. But as soon as Rubbi took over, Bannah revealed his sadistic, and murderous nature. We called him the angel of death because he frequently selected people for execution and then killed them himself. He usually made his choices during the daily march of Jewish workers from the camp to the base, which Bannah supervised. If, during the march, he saw a Jew who appeared to be weak or sick he would take him aside and shoot him on the spot with his rifle.

The men's and women's barracks in the Wolanow camp were located about two city blocks apart. Sometimes a number of the local Polish farmers would come into the camp and steal jewelry from the women's barracks, so the Jewish camp police set up a system of using volunteers to guard their barracks. One night, my brother Morrie was on this duty at one of the women's barracks when Bannah drove up accompanied by four Poles. They got out and entered the barrack, turned on the light, then Bannah shouted, "Achtung, achtung! I am Joseph Bannah, and you all know who I am. I am ordering you to do exactly what I tell you. If any of you disobey my orders you will be shot." He ordered all the women in the barrack to gather any jewelry that they had, to line up, and give it all to him. Then Bannah picked out the eight most attractive women in the barrack and ordered them over to the sleeping area where there were lots of bunk beds. He told the eight that they were required to have sex with the Poles. After beating them with a whip, which he always carried with him, Bannah then ordered each woman to get undressed and get onto a top bunk. Then, while Bannah looked on, four of the women were raped by the Poles. Then they raped the second group of four women. When they left, Bannah took all the jewelry with him.

While this was happening Morrie was trying to do what he could to break up the proceedings. He shouted at Bannah, "You must stop! You are doing something that is not right, that is against human nature." But all Bannah did was to order the Poles to beat up Morrie.

By that time Emerglik had heard the commotion and ordered some of the camp police to get over to the barrack. When they got there they found Morrie lying on the ground. He had been beaten so severely that he was having convulsions, his arms and legs shaking and twitching, and he was unconscious.

The police wrapped him in a blanket, and Emerglik had him brought to our house in the men's camp. All this time, I had been in the house and had no idea what was taking place. Suddenly they brought in my brother Morrie bleeding and bruised. By the time I saw him, his face was so swollen and so black and blue that at first I couldn't recognize him. He was unconscious and seemed to be in a coma.

While Emerglik was telling us what had happened, Bannah arrived at my home and screamed at him, "If any of you Jews whispers a word to any German at the base about what took place tonight, you and everyone else here will be dead within 48 hours. I want you to remember that I am Bannah and I am in charge of you Jews and have the power to do whatever I want."

As soon as Bannah left, we sent for the doctor. When he arrived he said, "Get me some 'spiritus' right away." Spiritus was very potent, almost pure alcohol. He ordered two strong men to take off his clothes and to rub him with the spiritus. After a while Morrie began to breathe more normally and the doctor looked relieved. He told me that now he thought Morrie would live.

The doctor had Morrie placed on a bed and he gave him several injections. By this time I was thinking that even though Bannah had threatened to kill anyone who reported what he had done, it wasn't just an idle threat. The risk had to be taken. If Bannah wasn't stopped soon, any chance we had of surviving the war as "workers" for the Germans would soon be gone. We would all be demoralized, and wouldn't have the determination to survive that most of us in the camp had until Busse left. I realized that I would have to take a stand. Of all the inmates, I had the easiest access to Rubbi. I would report what Bannah had done to Rubbi. If I was killed for that, I would rather die as a hero than as a sheep.

I found a friend, Berkowicz Yuma, and asked him if he would accompany me to the base. This was actually a very dangerous thing to do in the middle of the night when we were all restricted to the camp. I said to Yuma, "Look, I am going to go to Rubbi and report Bannah. You know what Bannah said. If I am shot, you could be shot as well." Yuma said, "Let's go. I've made up my mind. I've made up my mind, so help me God."

I said, "In order to get Rubbi to do something about Bannah, it isn't enough that they raped or that they robbed the Jewish women. That's done by Germans all the time. Instead, I'm going to tell Rubbi that when Bannah ordered this gang rape, he did it 'in the name of the Führer and the German people (des deutsches Folkes).'"

Yuma said to me, "How can you say such a thing? He never said that."

I said, "It's probably our only chance. The Nazis take invoking their Führer's name very seriously. If they find out we're lying they'll kill us for sure. But, at least, before I die I want to try to get rid of him."

We walked about one kilometer into the fields by the camp. It was difficult to walk because it was open, soft earth. It was very late and walking was not easy. We got tired and I said to Yuma, "It's so late, let's go back to the camp and not go to Rubbi after all." Yuma agreed to return and we walked back to the camp.

That night I couldn't sleep. I thought to myself, "If I don't get rid of Bannah, we all will be dead anyway. Even if they shoot me I'll still say that he ordered the rape of the women and the robbery of their jewelry 'in the name of the Führer and the German people' and that accusation will ultimately bury him."

At five A.M., as soon as it was light, I got out of bed, said goodbye to my mother, and left for the base. I arrived at the sentry post where one of the sentries shouted, "Halt" and demanded my pass. I told them that I was the Schneidermeister and gave them my pass. One of them screamed at me, "What in hell are you doing over here so early in the morning?"

I told him, "I have a great deal of work to do for the base commander, please let me through. I have to get it done right away." He said "OK" and let me in.

As soon as I entered I flew as if I had wings towards Rubbi's quarters. First, though, I had to pass through another sentry post near the central telephone office where Nathan David was working as a switchboard operator. For some strange reason, all the Germans there thought he was English and called him "David," which they thought was an English name. When I arrived at the post the guard recognized me as "David's brother" and let me pass. I went into the building housing the central switchboard and found Nathan David and, crying, told him about what had happened and how Morrie had nearly been killed. Then I told him that I was going to try to get Bannah arrested, even if it meant risking my own life.

Nathan David said, "What do you mean? Where are you going?"

"I'm going to Rubbi to accuse Bannah."

He wished me luck, and said goodbye, with tears in his eyes, knowing that if I failed, I would certainly be executed.

I made it to Rubbi's apartment. Toby had previously worked for Busse as a housekeeper and after Busse had left, Rubbi had kept her. So I first went to Toby's room. She was surprised to see me there so early in the morning and said, "Kiwa . . . What are you doing here?"

I told her what had happened and why I had to report Bannah to Rubbi. Then I asked her if she would go into Rubbi's room first and tell him about what had happened. I thought that since she already worked for Rubbi and was a woman, he might be willing to listen to her. I was afraid he would throw me out as soon as he saw me, "You are a woman and he won't get as angry when you wake him. So maybe you'll go in to see Rubbi and tell him what happened, and I will be behind you."

She became hysterical. I don't have the strength. I don't have the courage. I want to die!" she said.

"No! Don't talk like that," I said. "I will go."

When I got to Rubbi's room, I noticed the door was ajar. So I pushed it wider and stood looking at Rubbi's magnificent living quarters. Before I spoke, I thought of the biblical teachings about how Jews sacrificed their lives in those times, about the ten sages who were killed by the Romans, about Rabbi Akiba, and others. And I thought: "Now is my time to die as a hero."

I wasn't afraid to die, but I was scared of Rubbi. It was six in the morning and he was going to be furious when I woke him. I knocked on the door, but no one answered. He was asleep. Then I knocked again, harder, and Rubbi woke up. He shouted: "Wer ist das" (Who is that?).

I answered: "Herr Oberbauführer . . . it is your Schneidermeister."

"Der Schneidermeister?" he shouted. "Come in!" and then, angrily, "Are you crazy? You'd better have a good reason for waking me."

As I started to explain, I began to cry. "It's very important . . . I want to report to you what Bannah did last night at the women's labor camp. You are the one in charge over us and you are our father. So I came, that's why I'm here."

He said, "Don't cry . . . speak!"

I told him the story of how Bannah came into the barrack and told the girls, "I am here and order you to obey me in the name of the Führer and the German people, and in the name of the Third Reich. If you don't do exactly as I say, I will shoot you."

I told Rubbi that Bannah took jewelry from the women in the barrack and placed it all in a bucket, which he kept. Then I told him how Bannah had selected the eight most beautiful girls, ordered them to the back of the barrack then told them they had to have sex with the four Polish laborers he had brought with him.

When Rubbi heard the story he said: "I want you to know, that if I find that you are lying, in an hour from now I will shoot you."

I said, "Good."

He then jumped out of his bed, walked over to the telephone, got through to the central switchboard, and told the police to arrest Bannah immediately and have him brought to his quarters as soon as he was found. He also told them to seal off the base so that no one could go in or out and ordered the police to find the four Polish truck drivers who had participated in the rape. Then he told me to go into another room and said, "You wait until I get back." I was surprised that he didn't lock or even close the door.

I watched him get dressed. It took only a few minutes for him to put on his uniform, strap on his holster, and insert his gun.

The room had a window that faced the courtyard where the inmates of the camp assembled every morning to be assigned to their work. As I looked, I heard Bannah screaming at a woman and I saw him whipping her furiously. Just then two police on bicycles, with rifles slung over their shoulders, rode into the courtyard. The police got off their bikes, walked over to Bannah, and pointed their rifles at him. I later heard from my friend Meier Datron that when the police shouted, "Bannah, raise your hands!" Bannah turned pale and started to shake. They marched him towards Rubbi's quarters, as all the Jewish laborers looked on amazed at what was happening.

By then Rubbi was walking outside. The window was open. When Bannah and his police escort reached Rubbi, I heard him say, "You are under arrest." Then Rubbi placed the handcuffs on Bannah. Just then some other police arrived with three of the four Polish laborers who had accompanied Bannah the night before. They were all herded into Rubbi's quarters. Bannah was locked in one room and the Poles in another.

It was now about 6:45 in the morning. Rubbi called the Sicherheitsdienst in Radom and reported to the SS officer in charge that he had arrested Bannah for war crimes. At nine A.M., several Gestapo officers from the Sicherheitsdienst arrived to conduct a court martial in Rubbi's office. Present were a prosecutor, an attorney, and a judge. Then they brought in a gendarme to act as translator. Unfortunately, they didn't know that the killer was a friend of Bannah's. Bannah was brought in, followed by the three Poles. The fourth one had run away and hadn't yet been found. Rubbi opened the court martial and pointing to me, he addressed the judge, saying, "Meine liebe Herre, this man's name is Carl Rosenberg. He woke me in the morning and reported the criminal acts that Bannah, who you see over there, and four Poles, three of whom are here, committed. You may question Rosenberg about what Bannah did."

I looked around Rubbi's office. There were pictures of Hitler, Goebbels, Goering, and Himmler on the wall. The judge was sitting at Rubbi's desk, and he asked me if I wanted to answer his questions in Polish, in which case everything I said would be translated by the gendarme who was Bannah's friend. That didn't sound like a good idea, so I answered, "Your honor, I am able to speak German well and would like the privilege of addressing you myself without a translator."

That seemed to sit well with the judge, and he asked me to describe what occurred. After I finished he said, "Is it true that Bannah, when he walked into the women's barracks, used the words 'In the name of the Führer and the German people' when he robbed the women of their jewelry and when he ordered the eight women raped?"

"Yes, your honor," I replied.

"Did you hear him say these words yourself?" The camp police guards heard him and me.

Again I said, "Yes," even though I actually hadn't been there at the time.

The judge looked at me and said, "Do you know, if you are not telling the truth you will be shot?"

"Yes, I know that."

All of us—Rubbi, the Poles, and I—were at the front of the room. Rubbi was at my left.

After I finished, recounting the story, the prosecutor rose and said, "Herr Bannah, is what this man said true?"

Bannah was trembling and couldn't speak. Finally he said, "Honorable judges, I have to be truthful with you. I was drunk at the time and I remember nothing of what happened."

Then the attorney who was assigned to represent Bannah rose and pleaded that Bannah couldn't be prosecuted because he had been drunk.

The prosecutor argued that: "German soldiers were bleeding, and dying on the front lines. And here behind those lines is someone who is living in comfort and who, in the name of our Führer and the German people commits these crimes."

Now I could breathe more easily. My strategy had worked. The prosecutor wasn't even talking about the rapes that took place. His only concern seemed to be the words "In the name of the Führer and the German people" that they thought Bannah had used at the advent of the crimes.

The judge ordered Bannah to be taken away for interrogation, and then it was the Poles' turn. The gendarme translated for them. Their version of the story was that Bannah had told them to come with him, that they were going to "have a little fun" with the Jewish girls in the camp. The judge asked, "Do you remember what Bannah said?" The question was translated for them. Since the Poles couldn't understand German, they could only shrug their shoulders. They hadn't understood anything that Bannah said in German to the women in the barrack.

The three Poles were sentenced to concentration camps.

Then, Rubbi told me to "take a bicycle that Bannah used for work and get back to work at the tailor shop."

When I returned to the shop, everyone was jubilant. They lifted me up on their shoulders and said, "Where did you ever get the strength and the courage to do what you did?" By then word had spread all over the base, among the Germans, the Jews, and the Poles, about what I had done and how Bannah had been arrested.

I knew that Bannah had forced a young eighteen-year-old Jewish woman to be his mistress. She told me and my sister Toba that Bannah had buried all the jewelry he had stolen, under the floor of their house. I then told Rubbi about how it had been rumored that Bannah had stolen lots of jewelry from Jewish women who were on their way to concentration camps or who had been massacred, as had happened earlier at the Wolanow camp. I told Rubbi I was quite sure he had the booty hidden under the floorboards of his room. Sure enough, when Rubbi searched the room, he had some workers lift up the floorboards and they found Bannah's stash of stolen goods. I was sure that this had finally sealed Bannah's fate.

Several days later, Rubbi told me that he wanted to speak with the girls who had been raped. I immediately rushed to find them to tell them to be sure to tell Rubbi about the words, "In the name of the Führer and the German people," that Bannah was supposed to have said. I told them to be sure to remember, because if they didn't I would be killed, and if I was killed, they probably would suffer the same fate. I needn't have worried. They gave the proper version of the story and shortly afterwards Bannah was sentenced. They kept him 4 weeks for interrogation in the gendarmes station, in the cellar. My friend Szmulek the red[1] had Sznistowski act as caretaker for Bannah. Szmulek was the master at taking care of the horses at the Zandamms station. Bannah was in hell already. Szmulek survived and lives in Canada as well as the U.S.A.

He was given the choice of being shot or sent to the Russian front. He chose the Russian front. Three months later, Rubbi called me into his office and asked

---

1. Szmulek probably had red hair. —Editor's note

me, "Do you want to know what happened to Bannah?" I nodded, so he opened a file cabinet and showed me a document stating that Bannah had been killed at the front.

Actually Bannah's being away may have saved my life. Another Jew told me that Bannah was planning to "get rid of the Rosenberg family the first chance I get." He would have gotten his opportunity two months later, when Rubbi went to Stuttgart for the Christmas holidays. If Bannah had remained at the camp, he would have been in charge of all of us while Rubbi was gone.

## chapter 12

Although I had fully recovered from my own bout with typhus, an epidemic of the disease spread through the camp and, several weeks later, into the surrounding area. This was in December of 1942. The province's health department officials believed the camp's inmates were the source of the typhus and quarantined the camp. Signs were posted throughout the camp declaring that all occupants were assumed to be infected with typhus; no one entering the camp would be allowed to leave. Quarantine was usually a precursor to certain execution. The Germans had good reason to fear an epidemic. The disease is highly contagious and usually causes a fever of one hundred five degrees, this followed by chills, head and backaches, nausea, and, finally, delirium. The fatality rate in those days was close to twenty percent, and those who survived were left in a weakened state for a long time.

Every Jew in the camp understood the Nazis' logic. According to them, all Jews were vermin, like lice. These carry typhus. Therefore, the epidemic was the fault of the Jews.

When the Nazis quarantined the camp, rumors began to spread that the eight hundred and fifty inmates of the camp were doomed, even though most were not sick. A way had to be found to save at least some, if not most of us. I was one of six people designated by the other members of the camp as a planning committee.

By that time the Germans were beginning to lose the war. They had run into stiff resistance at Stalingrad, and we began to hear rumors of other German military setbacks. The news of these losses obviously disturbed the Germans stationed in Poland. We doubted that they would have much patience with Polish Jews who contracted a disease for which there was no known cure. We feared that they would probably try to get rid of the problem by disposing of us.

Late one afternoon in early January 1943, a group of six of us met to discuss the situation and decide if anything could be done about it. Our committee was aware of rumors that the Germans were planning to have all the Jews in the camp shot in order to wipe out the epidemic. In fact, there were only twenty-five cases of typhus and five or six with influenza or pneumonia out of a total of eight hundred and fifty prisoners in the camp. Among those with typhus, many were on the verge of death.

We decided that we would wait and see if Rubbi would countermand the quarantine order and allow certain key workers at the air base to leave the camp to go to work. Then, any of us who were able to get out would approach Rubbi and try to convince him that the typhus epidemic wasn't that serious, and that it could be controlled without killing the inmates. To give Rubbi more reason to listen to us, the committee was ready to draw from the camp bribe fund, which consisted of what remaining valuables we had collected for just such an emergency. Some of the collection came from contributions, but much of it derived from the belongings of two Jewish women who had been murdered the previous fall.

At that time, a young Pole, who hunted Jews for the Nazi bounty, seized a wealthy woman and her teenage daughter. The women had been hiding in the forest, hoping to join the imprisoned Jews in the Wolanow camp. Although it was a labor camp, it was still safer than trying to survive by hiding among the hostile Christian communities outside. It was common practice for Catholic Poles to hunt Jews. The Nazis offered two kilograms of sugar, five kilos of salt, and twenty liters of kerosene for every Jew caught, no matter what his or her age.

In the case of the two women, the young Pole raped the daughter in front of her mother, then turned them over to the gendarmes to claim his reward. The women were held overnight, and, in the morning, were taken to a deserted shack alongside an open grave. The mother begged to be shot first, but they killed the daughter first, and the mother had to watch her daughter die, and then, she was shot. Although they were looking for booty, both the fortune hunter and the gendarmes overlooked the valuables which the women had sewn into their brassieres. Prisoners from the camp were detailed to bury them and discovered the money and jewels, which they turned over to the committee.

At midmorning the day after the committee meeting, two "black traitors" approached our compound and told the camp police to fetch me. I was taken directly to Rubbi's office. "I've got lots of work for you," he said, "and I don't want you in the camp!" He seemed to imply that everyone else in the camp would be killed soon, and he wanted me to stay around to do his tailoring. I worked on his uniforms for a while until I had a chance to speak with him alone. I asked him if he would do me a big favor. Would he give me permission to reenter the camp to say goodbye to my mother? Rubbi didn't like the idea but relented when I asked him if he wouldn't have wanted to do the same thing if he were in my shoes.

I went back and visited my mother and told her that all hope was not yet gone. Then I visited one of our committee members, using the excuse that I was retrieving some tools I'd left behind. He had the bribe prepared in a small sack which I hid in my pants. Once back at the base, I immediately went to Rubbi's quarters. "What's on your mind?" Rubbi asked.

I told him how much I appreciated his generosity in allowing me to see my mother and that I had one other very important matter to talk about. "Let's hear it," he said. I presented the small sack, saying, "I have brought something for you." He wanted to know what it was, and I said it was for his wife. Rubbi looked into the sack, and his face seemed to brighten a little. The sack contained some five thousand dollars worth of gold and jewelry.

There was a faint sparkle in Rubbi's eyes as he examined the contents and calculated its worth. Then he quickly put the sack out of sight and warned me that "no one else should ever know about this little secret." I assured him that the secret was safe with me. "You are the only one who can save the people in the camp," I told him. "They don't deserve to die, and with very few exceptions they certainly are not sick with typhus. Think of yourself, Herr Rubbi. Those people in the camp are your workforce. If they are liquidated, isn't it possible that your usefulness here will be finished, and that they would send you somewhere else?" It's quite possible. Every day the Germans were sending more and more men to fight their losing battles on the Russian front.

"As a wise man," I said, "we believe that you don't really intend to be the cause of your own downfall." Rubbi understood exactly what I was getting at; he asked what I had to suggest. I assured him that they could contain the epidemic without killing the inmates.

I suggested that he call the area headquarters of the German civil authority, the SD or *Sicherheitsdienst*, in Radom, outline the situation to his superiors, and ask them to reconsider the liquidation plan. After all, he could point out, the problem was really a lot worse outside the camp in the Christian sections of the surrounding area, than inside, where only a very small number had typhus. I also suggested that he offer to have the camp inspected by the health department. We were ready to hide all the sick people and keep them away from the barrack area.

Rubbi agreed to try to save the camp, but first, he insisted, he would have the camp purged of all sick people. By "purge" Rubbi meant to liquidate all the sick Jews in the camp. Only when the "purge" was completed would he seek relief from the quarantine and the inevitable death sentence attached to it. He said he wanted to present a healthy Jewish population for the inspector. Then he telephoned the SD *Obersturmbannführer* to make the initial arrangements to countermand the liquidation order. The SD officials in Radom accepted Rubbi's plan and gave him permission to deal directly with the health department to arrange for an inspector to come to the camp.

I reported on my discussion with Rubbi to our committee. Of all the people who were sick, most of them were beyond recovery and could not be moved. Even if they could, it was impossible to find places to hide them all. I knew of only one ill woman who was hidden in the attic of an abandoned farmhouse on the campgrounds. She was kept warm with some blankets and left to fend for herself for most of the time she was in hiding. There may have been others, but I didn't know any of the details; I suspected their friends and families kept it secret, even from the other camp inmates. We had to face the reality that those who were too sick to be moved to hiding places would either have to get well in a hurry or be killed by the Germans.

On Rubbi's orders, Barkmann made an inspection of the camp, wrote down the names of all the sick inmates, and had them all transferred to one barrack. Then he brought arsenic compound to the barrack and ordered a doctor to give a fatal injection to each of the sick ones. There was not the slightest doubt that, if he didn't comply, this doctor, who had been doing his best to treat the same sick Jewish inmates and to allow them to live, would be shot immediately, along with the typhus victims and possibly the rest of the camp's population. The dead were buried immediately. When he heard Barkmann's report that all was "in order," Rubbi called the health department and invited them to inspect the Wolanow camp.

The Christian Polish doctor who was the medical health inspector for the region made his tour of the camp. Nothing was found amiss. There was no sickness nor any symptoms of typhus found among the inmates. just to make sure the inspector was not confused about what he had seen, we gave him a few thousand zlotys—about one hundred dollars.

The health department doctor reported the camp to be free of typhus, and trucks began delivering food rations, which had been cut off during the quarantine. The trucks were a good sign to our people and morale began to improve. Even so, a three week quarantine was maintained for those who worked outside the camp, just to be sure.

During the quarantine, I had been ordered to set up shop in Rubbi's living quarters at the air base. My father, my two brothers, and my sister, Toba, were also with me, as they each had jobs at the base. We all stayed in an unoccupied section of Rubbi's quarters. My mother, who worked in the camp kitchen, hadn't been allowed to leave.

Rubbi was not taking any chances with typhus. He made us take delousing showers shortly after we arrived. Jews weren't normally allowed to take hot showers or to obtain the delousing antiseptics. For the first time in a very long time, we were vermin-free and clean.

One of the problems I had in Rubbi's quarters during the quarantine was that there were no latrine facilities that I could use. There were nearly one hundred and fifty Germans living in the apartmentlike quarters. Normally, two latrines were provided: one for Jews and one for everyone else. Signs were posted at the entrances which warned Jews that they would be punished if they used the wrong facility. The punishment was at the least a beating and sometimes even death. The problem was, that in Rubbi's building there weren't any facilities for Jews.

Rubbi personally warned me not to use the latrines when any German officers were about. As a result, during the three weeks of quarantine, I suffered. Late at night when almost everyone was asleep I would occasionally dare to use the indoor toilet. Sometimes I would sneak down the corridor during supper to use the toilet. After eating dinner, the Germans usually drank heavily and went to sleep drunk. Some of them would even give me beer every now and then.

At the end of the three week precautionary quarantine, there still was no sign of typhus. So the quarantine was lifted and the status of the inmates returned to "normal." We were still prisoners, but many of the restrictions had been relaxed. At that time my father, brothers, sister, and I, who had been staying at the air base, returned to our house in the camp to be reunited with my mother.

During the three weeks of isolation, I listened to several radio broadcasts over a receiver in Rubbi's communications center. Some of them were clearly from the Russian front. First there was music, then a voice speaking in German, with a Russian accent. The voices would be telling their listeners that the Germans should stop fighting at once in order to save thousands and thousands of lives. Then the music would come back on, and I heard voices that seemed to be coming from German soldiers sending messages to their families in their homeland. I often could identify the sounds of war in the background—artillery fire blocked out some of the words of the soldiers' messages. I believe they may have been part of General Paulus' army, which was trying to capture Stalingrad.

From time to time, the broadcasts would be interrupted by another transmitter with a station identification of "Radio Moscow." The announcer said, "This message is to the German people. We want you to know that the armies commanded by General Paulus must surrender. There is no way for them to survive if they do not surrender." My blood ran cold. I was afraid that one of Rubbi's men might discover my eavesdropping. There was no telling what might happen if they discovered that I or any other Jews from the camp knew of the difficulties the Germans were suffering on the Russian front. For me, though, it was worth the risk of discovery to hear that the enemy was suffering such big losses.

Radio Moscow also appealed to the German soldiers to lay down their arms. "On the Russian front," they said, "all is lost for the Germans." I didn't stop to consider whether the Radio Moscow broadcast was true. It thrilled me more than I can say to think of the downfall of the Nazi regime. Listening to that broadcast was a glorious and uplifting moment for me.

◆ ◆ ◆

When the German offensive against Stalingrad failed, all activities on the base came to a standstill. The theater closed, and all entertainment was suspended. The ranking officers also grew beards. When I asked Rubbi why he hadn't shaved, he said, "We are in national mourning because of the failure at Stalingrad." There had been a similar eight day mourning period when the *Bismarck* was sunk in 1941.

◆ ◆ ◆

One day thirty Jewish men were brought from Radom to work in the base lumberyards. By some mistake, they were taken to our camp, and someone decided that they had been brought there for execution. A Ukrainian death squad was summoned. As the Ukrainians were preparing for the slaughter, Clara Landau, the Jewish secretary of Mr. Jordan, the labor administrator on the base, told me, "Carl, you know thirty men were supposed to have come to the base to do some extra work in the lumberyard today. The men have been taken to the camp by mistake. I just saw them pass through the base on the way to the camp and the Ukrainians will probably kill them when they get there."

I immediately rushed off to call Jordan and told him about the mix-up and the threat to the workers' lives. I pleaded with him to "please, rush over to the camp and save them." Because there was no way to communicate with the camp, other than by going there in person or sending a courier, Jordan took his three-wheeled motorized cart and went there. The moment he arrived he discovered that the Ukrainians were doing exactly what we had feared. After a severe beating, the thirty workers had been marched at bayonet point to a pit grave located some three hundred yards off the road. Jordan stopped the execution and sent the workers back to the base for first aid. Clara Landau and I patched their wounds and bandaged their broken bones with supplies which Jordan gave us. A few of the most severely wounded stayed at the tailor shop where it was nice and warm. Those who were able were required to work for eight more days. Then the whole group was sent back to Radom.

The free-roaming Ukrainian murderers were commanded by an *Oberscharführer* named Kappka. This group was in charge of all the shooting and murdering of Jews in the district that included Radom, Wolanow, and the surrounding areas. One Sunday in April of 1943, I saw a truck drive into camp. In the back of the truck were fifteen Jews, along with several Ukrainians. In the cab was a driver and a German officer, none other than Oberscharführer Kappka. When I saw them arrive I knew that there would be trouble so I quickly went into my house and upstairs to a window where I could inconspicuously watch what was happening.

I saw Kappka get out and shout orders at the Ukrainians who jumped off the truck. Then the Jews got off and were marched to a small, gently sloping hill. I could hear Kappka scream at them to take off their clothes, but they refused. Kappka and the Ukrainians beat them until blood ran from their wounds, particularly on their faces and heads, and the Jews finally begged them to stop and started taking off their clothes. Kappka then lined them up in single file one person standing right up against the other person. He then walked behind the last person in the line, pulled out his pistol, aimed it at this last person's back and shot the entire line with one short burst from his automatic gun. The entire line of men fell forward simultaneously like a stack of dominoes. The Jewish police were then ordered to bury the dead in a mass grave.

I later learned the men in the truck were Jewish intellectuals and leaders from the Radom ghetto. It was at the time of the Warsaw Ghetto Uprising and the Germans were worried that the same thing could happen in the many ghettos located in other large cities in Poland, so they decided to execute any Jew who seemed competent enough to serve as a leader for any potential uprising.

Kappka survived the war. I learned that the German government had considered trying him for war crimes, but he was too ill to stand trial.

Civilians of Nuremberg, both men and women, participate in carrying the bodies of slave laborers a mile and a half outside of the city of Nuremberg for burial.

Civilians of Nuremberg, Germany, carry the bodies of slave laborers a mile and a half outside of the city for burial.

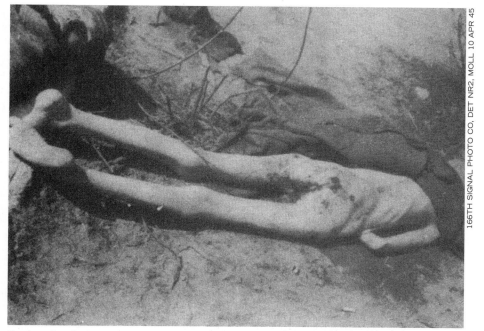

Body of a victim, which had been lying in this position for about a week before the Americans overran the camp of Ohrdruf. One of many who were brutally shot by the Nazis.

Bodies of Allied prisoners, Russian, American, French, Polish, and numerous other nationalities await burial by civilians at the Schwarzenfeld concentration camp, Germany.

Bodies of old men and young kids in the mass grave at the concentration camp near Buchenwald, Germany.

At the burial grounds outside Nuremberg, Germany, a prayer was offered in English, Polish, and German for the slave laborers who had been murdered by the Nazis.

Jewish women, who died from brutality and malnutrition, lying in the field awaiting burial by civilians at the Hergenhein concentration camp, Germany.

Bodies of the victims stacked like cord wood waiting to be cremated or buried in a grave of hundreds, Ohrdruf, Germany. The white substance is lime, for the sake of smell.

Civilians digging graves for the bodies of Allied prisoners of all nationalities at the prison camp in Schwarzenfeld, Germany.

Bodies of the men and kids stacked outside the building in which they will be cremated in large furnaces at Buchenwald concentration camp.

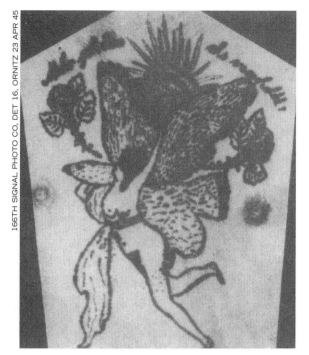

This tattoo was part of a man's body until it was skinned off by Nazi SS men and used as a decoration on the wall of their quarters at Buchenwald concentration camp.

Bodies of the men who were taken from the mass grave at Wetterfeld, Germany, lying alongside the grave. There were 59 bodies in the grave, civilians are digging them out.

This man being helped along by his friends is so weak from lack of food that he can hardly walk. One of the many hundreds in the same condition at the Buchenwald camp near Weimar, Germany.

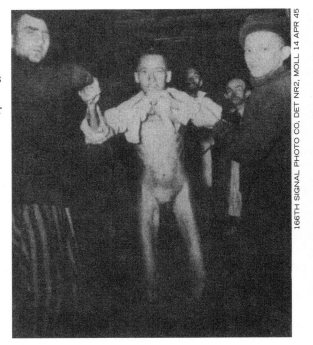

This photo shows the conditions and the amount of sleeping space for the prisoners at Buchenwald concentration camp. They range from young kids to old men, all doing the same amount of work each day.

Day of Liberation

Three of the luckier ones upon liberation.

Post liberation underground training in Landsberg for future service in the Israeli Army.

Our first temporary synagogue after liberation. Many grateful prayers were offered by the fortunate ones.

# chapter 13

Later in April of 1943, shortly after the murder of the fifteen intellectuals, the Wolanow camp was liquidated. Rubbi told me that there was nothing he could do to keep any Jews on the base. He said that an order had come through Himmler in the German High Command requesting that all Jews remaining in any ghetto or employed at any military bases had to be transported to concentration camps that were administered by the SS. Eichmann was to be in charge of the disposition of all of those Jews. He warned me that conditions in camps administered by the SS were much worse than anything I could imagine and that it would be a miracle if I survived.

The inmates from the Wolanow camp were to be transported to a concentration camp located in Blizyn. I was worried that we might be forced to march to the train station in Radom, some fifteen kilometers away and that a few of us would not survive such a march because we would be attacked by the free-roaming Ukrainian murderers along the way. I begged Rubbi to arrange for a safe transport. Rubbi was willing to help us this one last time. He ordered trucks to carry us to the central train station in Radom where we were loaded onto cattle cars and taken away to Blizyn, a subsidiary of the Lublin-Majdanek camp, located in the Kielce district, about twenty-five kilometers from Starachowice. We stayed at Blizyn until June 1944.

During the liquidation of the ghettos, about fifty-five hundred people were transferred to Blizyn from many parts of Poland. It was a vile place with a very strong security system. It must have been built to handle the very worst kind of criminals. We slept in horse barns on cement slabs—men segregated from women. Some of the slabs were so close to the floor that a person could easily crack a shin if he wasn't careful walking around after dark. Everyone had to work sixteen hours a day.

The discipline was very harsh and cruel. We were whipped and starved. People were shot for breaking even the most trivial rules. Our work consisted of mass-production tailoring. Five hundred of us worked on the day shift and another five hundred on the night, sewing SS winter uniforms and camouflage combat uniforms one side of which was green, the other white.

Each time we left the labor area we were searched for contraband. The Germans were afraid that we would steal bobbins or needles. In the process of trying to reach our quota of eight to ten uniforms a day, a person might easily forget that he had hastily slipped a bobbin into his pocket. We soon learned to remember such things. Walking out of the door with a bobbin in your pocket was considered sabotage and anyone caught was shot. There was no mercy, even if the guilty party had only committed an honest oversight.

The punishment for breaking a needle on the sewing machines could also be death. There were "rules" posted everywhere. I saw a few unfortunate tailors who broke sewing machine needles shot after being read a statement that they had committed "sabotage." There weren't a large number of such executions—only enough to convince the rest of us to take the rules seriously.

One day, about three hundred of us were ordered to march toward a barrack. Then, as we stood in front of the barrack, we were told that it had been fumigated with poisonous gas and that we would be running in it to take out field uniforms that had been placed inside earlier, before the fumigation began. The guards opened the doors of the barrack and ordered ten prisoners to run in the door, grab the clothes, and then run out of the same door. When they emerged, it was the turn of the next ten. When I was supposed to enter, I took a deep breath before going into the barrack, ran over to a rack where German uniforms were hanging, and then ran out as fast as I could, while holding my breath. Even though I wasn't breathing, I began to get dizzy, and I fell down as I was going outside. But I arose and, once outside, took some deep breaths. I was lucky. The fumigant was none other than the Zyklon-B gas that was used in the extermination camps. There was enough of it in the barrack to kill four of our group of three hundred while trying to get the uniforms.

Later we were assigned the task of cleaning and repairing those uniforms. They had obviously been removed from dead soldiers at the Russian front. There were bullet holes through many of them, along with parts of soldiers' bodies. It was a macabre experience, finding isolated human fingers, toes, even ears, lying in the folds of the fabric. We also found many letters, usually addressed to a soldier's parents. I read all of the letters I came across, hoping to get some news. In most instances the soldier was complaining about the war, about how the Germans were losing the war on the Russian front, and asking questions like, "Why do we have to die in a war when it wasn't necessary for Hitler to invade Russia." After reading these letters we destroyed them. As slave laborers, we weren't allowed to know about German defeats. We were supposed to believe in German invincibility, just like the "dupes" that allowed Hitler's rise to power. Yet the letters we found in the bullet-riddled uniforms were more confirming evidence that the war was going poorly for Germany and that there was hope that we might survive this nightmare, if only we could stay alive.

Because of the horrendous conditions at Blizyn, some of the inmates tried to escape and a number actually succeeded in running away. After several escapes, Obersturmbannführer Nell, the commander of the Blizyn camp, ordered that the three men who shared each bunk should be chained together at night. This would make it almost impossible for anyone to get away. But prisoners found ways of breaking the chains and there were still more escapes. So Nell ruled that if anyone of a group of three fled the other two would be held responsible and would be killed as punishment.

While I was at Blizyn I met Solomon Blumberg and his brother, whose name I don't remember. They were professional tailors in their early thirties who had been transported from Pietrkow Tribunaslsk. I'm not sure if they survived Auschwitz, their destination after Blizyn, which makes my recalling the story they told me probably the only record of their experiences.

They were in Pietrkow Tribunaslsk and were called by the Germans to join ten other Jews for a work party to clean out the latrines. The Germans, unhappy with the way the Jews were doing that filthy job, ordered Blumberg, his brother, and some of the other workers to eat the waste. The men at first refused to obey the order, but after they were beaten and kicked, they complied. Even so, two of the twelve workers refused. They were immediately shot and buried in the trench with the waste from the latrines. Later the survivors were allowed to wash their hands and faces, but that did not relieve the stench their bodies and minds had absorbed from the disgusting ordeal. Blumberg said that it was more terrible than any torture he had ever thought possible, and that the man who forced them to eat the feces thought it was a great joke. According to Blumberg, the German told them, "You have to eat our waste because you are Jews."

I have always wondered why the rest of the world stood idly by, allowing the

Jews to suffer so much. Although we did not know if reports reached the rest of the world at the time we were prisoners, there were indeed reports that were issued as early as 1941. These stated that Jews were being systematically murdered by the Germans and presented facts and figures.

The meager coverage in the press of Great Britain and the United States did little for those of us in the camps. Even in there we heard about the atrocities through the Polish underground. While in Wolanow and in Blizyn, I received news from Christian contacts outside the camps who were in the underground and who repeated what they had heard over shortwave radios from England. They also gave me a leaflet that described some of the facts that had already been accumulated about the Nazi extermination policy and the death camps.

◆ ◆ ◆

In May of 1944, the Russians, along with remnants of the Polish army, began to move against the Germans. In one of their first advances, they drove the enemy back almost to Warsaw. Then the Poles broke the German lines and recaptured Lublin, only about forty kilometers from Blizyn. We heard shooting all night long and thought we might be liberated then and there. It was, however, a vain hope. Early one morning we were told that we should prepare to be relocated from Blizyn. But when the time came to move, there were too few cattle cars, so we stayed. Others had already been transported out of the camp, including my father. We heard that he had been taken to another camp somewhere in Poland, but we didn't know where.

Meanwhile there were encouraging signs. We noticed that the Germans, particularly the SS men, were taking shelter in our camp. They showed the scars of very hard battles. Their uniforms were torn and dirty, and the men themselves had not washed or shaved for a long time.

One day, some German refugees arrived with their families. They brought with them horses, buggies, chickens, and goats. We also saw many German soldiers. It was obvious that these men had just come back from fighting the Russians. They wore ragged uniforms, and many of them were bandaged. They were tired and exhausted and we were sure they had just made a hasty retreat, probably on foot, from the Russian positions. At that point, a number of us began to think that the German power had been broken and the "Heroes" were definitely losing the war.

Based on that assumption, the logical thing to do was to plan an uprising. We would kill the watchmen posted on the towers around the camp. They were all Ukrainians who carried weapons and killed whenever they felt like it. If the Germans were really being pushed back, there was no telling how the Ukrainians might react.

Then in June, much to our dismay, the sound of shooting in the distance died down, and three days later the Germans brought in a train with cattle cars for our transportation out of Blizyn. We were ordered to pack up the sewing machines and other equipment, and we were loaded abruptly onto the cattle cars.

It was now June of 1944. Twenty-five SS men armed with heavy machine guns and accompanied by German shepherd dogs traveled with us. Ukrainians, Lithuanians, Latvians, and Estonians were used as guards in that transport. Before boarding the train all those who were sick were separated from the rest of us and taken to a wooded area just outside the camp and shot. Normally they would have been treated at a first aid station, but it had been razed because we were moving out of the camp.

Before we were loaded into the cars, we were ordered to remove our civilian clothes and were given striped uniforms. Besides the SS guards, there were also the usual Ukrainians on every car. Machine guns were mounted on the roofs and between the loading ramps leading into the cars. There was no doubt that anyone who tried to escape would be killed. It was the middle of the day by the time the train was fully loaded and began to move. There were two locomotives, one in the front and one in the rear, probably because it was such a heavy load.

During my stay at Blizyn many of the original fifty-five hundred Jews had been killed by the Germans or had died of illness and injuries. As a result, only about thirty-five hundred Jews boarded the train. Although some of the cars were packed with more than a hundred people, most of them had eighty to ninety to a car. The guards usually closed the door when all the floor space of the car was fully occupied.

There was only a tiny window in one wall, close to the roof, and it was equipped with iron bars. The doors were locked from the outside. Because of the crowding, the air was very bad, and there was no food or water. We had no idea as to where we were going, but perhaps it was just as well. If we had known, we would surely have panicked.

We posted a lookout to watch through the little window. He stood on the shoulders of another prisoner so he could see out of the window. By keeping track of the cities we passed, we knew when we had arrived at Chenstohawa, a large city in Poland. There the train stopped. We waited on a siding for about four hours. While at this stop, we were given a little food and water. I thought that if we only could have slipped away from the cattle cars, we would have had a good chance of escaping. But with all the guards and wearing our conspicuous striped uniforms, that was only wishful thinking.

Eventually the train started to move again. From time to time, we passed through dense forests. Ever so often Polish partisans would fire their machine guns at us from the cover of the heavy timber. Whenever we passed a wooded area there would be lots of shooting. The bullets penetrated the walls, and we had to huddle on the floor for safety. After a while, the walls were riddled with bullet holes. But the train kept moving and no one in our car was hit.

# chapter 14

Two days after we left Blizyn, we arrived at Auschwitz. By then, twenty-five of the prisoners in our car alone, had died. Their bodies were stacked at one end of the railroad car to give the rest of us more room to move. The train stopped on a siding. As we waited to be unloaded, we knew nothing about Auschwitz, but we soon became aware of an odor more serious than that of the stench of human waste that permeated the cattle car. It was the odor of cooking meat. It was putrid, but it made us very curious.

As the cars were opened, we saw SS men standing everywhere. They were yelling, *"raus, raus"* and *"schnell, schnell."* From the beginning, we knew that this camp was different from Blizyn. The putrid odor was all pervasive. Then we noticed chimneys rising from a row of buildings that resembled the factories of Warsaw.

"Transport Kommandos"—inmates who had been assigned to help process the new arrivals at the camp, assisted the SS as they ordered us to *"springen"* or jump down from the train. Shouting, the transport kommandos ordered those already on the ground to line up in a hurry. It was dangerous to jump from the car because the SS were waiting to club anyone who didn't land on his feet. The Germans used heavy rubber nightsticks, and they seemed determined to club as many prisoners as possible. Once everyone was out, the transport kommandos scurried inside to clean up the dead. The unloading was swift and methodical. It was clear that we were not the first prisoners to arrive at Auschwitz.

"Line up, line up," came the orders. "Women over here in a line at the right," the guards shouted. There weren't any children with us, though we had some adult-sized teenagers who were fifteen or sixteen years old. The oldest in our group was about forty.

One of the guards shouted *"Achtung!"* and a man of about twenty-seven or twenty-eight came into view. He seemed to be at least six-feet-two tall and I remember that his face was white, unblemished, and innocent looking compared to those guards. He looked quite healthy and strong, but his eyes were penetrating and incredibly sharp without any trace of compassion. This man ordered the other SS men to march our group towards the gates leading into that industrial-looking area with the low buildings and large chimneys. I didn't see any smoke rising from the chimneys, but the odor of burning flesh was everywhere.

I was pretty sure that none of the prisoners who had just arrived knew what was about to happen to us, although I sensed that there was great danger. The guards were very cautious in handling us, as if they were trying to avoid giving us any reason to panic. That only confirmed my fears. "Don't move from the lines or you will be shot on the spot," the guards warned. We didn't move.

Later I learned that the impressive young German with the innocent appearance was Dr. Joseph Mengele, who has been called by many survivors of Auschwitz the "angel of death."

Mengele and another officer stood at the head of the columns we had formed, and they started looking for sick people. The ill and those who looked as if they might not be strong enough to work, were shoved aside. Some of those were not really sick. They were just depressed, and that was all that really mattered.

After the first selection had been made, an officer handed Mengele a letter which must have described our working ability. Perhaps it was from the commandant at Blizyn, *Obersturmführer* Nell. After Mengele read the contents, he ordered the sick, weak, and depressed-looking to the left; all the others were sent to the right. We didn't know what that meant, but later we learned that those who went to the left were gassed and burned in the ovens. I remember very well what Mengele sounded like as he ordered "left" and "right." His voice was characterized by a cold Germanic precision and arrogance. After a while he asked another officer to take over, telling him to "make it short."

We could see that the selection process had removed most of those who were too sick or weak to do heavy work. All during this tense time there was music. An orchestra of about forty people was playing, the male musicians on one side, female on the other. It was strange to see this group playing music for an audience composed only of the newly arrived prisoners.

My mother, my sister, Toba, and my brother, Nathan David, arrived at Auschwitz at the same time that I did. Those of us who had been ordered to go to the right had to wait outdoors all through the night. We were waiting for showers. During the long wait we had an opportunity to talk with some of the inmates who had been working in the area. They told us about the gas chambers and how they disguised them as showers. Whenever prisoners were taken to the showers they could be going to real showers or to the gas chambers. Both were in the same general location and both appeared the same with similar signs on the outside, and we could see long lines heading into the entrance of what we had been told was where the gas chambers were located. At this point we had no way of knowing whether we would actually get a shower or be gassed. We spent the night wondering what would happen to us. Our naked bodies were shivering from the cold winds.

After a long wait, we were marched to the shower area. During the march SS men were screaming at us and beating anyone who was slow. We entered a building and were told to move into a large room. Many of the first few in line thought that they might be entering a gas chamber and shivered with fear. The guards hit them with rubber nightsticks, whips, and sometimes with the butt of a gun. Finally they had about five hundred of us packed in the shower room, and they turned on the cold water.

After the shower came the disinfection process. Chemicals, which burned our skin and seemed to remove our body hair, were splashed on us. It was terrible. Then, we were given new striped uniforms and left to assume that we would never again see any of the few possessions that we brought with us.

After dressing, we were ordered to form two long columns and marched away from the shower and disinfecting station. We headed for the barracks where we would be "quarantined" for a while.

Actually it was merely temporary housing for us until we could be integrated into the routine of the camp. About eight hundred of us were forced into one barrack. Most could talk only about the chances of being selected for the gas chambers.

"Where is God to help us?" I thought. "Why has God forsaken us? If we must die at the hands of these German brutes, will the whole world accept the pain and burden of responsibility for our deaths, or will we be like cattle in the slaughterhouse—no regrets by anyone?"

A few days later we were ordered to turn over all valuables we may have retained. What a ludicrous request, considering the fact that by this time we had no valuables left. Barrack Number Ten, to which I had been assigned, had a loudspeaker, and the person giving the orders said that we should drop all valuables into boxes which the kapos would pass around. The kapos were inmates who were assigned to the role of camp enforcers. In general they were cruel and sadistic, thinking nothing of beating someone's head for their exercise! It was all very baffling, and it confirmed our suspicion that Auschwitz wasn't really a work camp. As yet, there had been no mention of labor.

The loudspeaker voice continued: "All men are here to work. Our slogan is *Arbeit macht das Leiden frei* (work will set you free). And just in case you do not understand where you are, you are in Auschwitz. Nobody escapes from here. If you do not work, you will leave through the chimneys. If you work hard to help the Third Reich achieve victory, which is being won now, then mercy may be extended to you." My brother, Nathan David, and I were assigned to the same barrack. After listening to the voice over the loudspeaker, he told me that he was sure we were going to die.

Even with such dire prospects, the spirits of my fellow prisoners were not completely broken. Instead of surrendering their few remaining valuables, many of the men hid what they had in the darkest recesses of the buildings. I don't know how they had managed to keep anything during the shower and delousing process, but some did. Maybe they swallowed some of the small valuables and vomited them up later.

While I was at Auschwitz I wasn't assigned to any regular job. On a few occasions, I worked with several others on the maintenance of the barracks. But the rest of the time I stayed around my barrack waiting to see what would happen.

One day the SS came into the barrack, made a selection, and Nathan David was taken away. I tried to follow him but an SS man knocked me to the ground and I was forced to remain. Nathan David was transferred to another barrack and was made a Transport Kommando. Once he was gone, I had little contact with him. My mother was given a job in the kitchen. Toba volunteered for work outside of Auschwitz and was put on a transport and shipped out of the camp.

New trainloads were arriving all the time. I remember that some of the trains were from Holland. Sometimes the new arrivals came in regular passenger cars, and had no idea what awaited them. They probably thought Auschwitz was a work camp. Day after day I saw the new inmates lined up; wives in one line, husbands in another, and children split between them. Some went left, some went right, and after a few hours, the chimneys began to emit smoke.

The world we lived in was strange. We were able to keep track of the calendar because inmate musicians were required to perform on Sundays. A women's choir would sing *a cappella*. The musicians also played for the new arrivals so they wouldn't suspect that they were about to be murdered. The best ones played for the German officers on Sunday, but inmates were also allowed to listen. They played Tchaikowsky, Beethoven, and others. They would play for a couple of hours, and the breaks in the program were filled with other entertainment such as magicians and jugglers.

The barracks had no windows. It was very dark, and light entered only through cracks between the roof and the walls. Everyday through the cracks, we could see the smoke rising from the chimneys. We wondered when our time to die would come.

Every day when the ovens started to burn the corpses, the chimneys would emit a very heavy dark smoke. Usually it started about eight in the morning. There were five chimneys but not all were belching smoke at the same time. After a couple of hours the smoke mixed with flames which shot up into the sky like the tail of a rocket. No sane person could absorb these facts and expect to live without divine intervention. We were aware that there had been no such intervention for all the thousands who had "left through the chimneys" before us. Why should we expect to be treated any differently?

To add to the horror of having to wait for our deaths, living conditions were indescribable. The barrack structures had originally been built as horse barns in which shelves had been installed. There were at least three shelves in each stall, and we had to sleep on our sides so that more people could be housed in each building. I slept on a ledge with thirty others. We had no mattresses and slept on rough wood slabs. For covers we had blankets of coarse wool, used for horses.

None of the barracks had toilet facilities. At night we were provided with two barrels—one for urine and another for feces—located at the west end of the barrack. The supervisor, called the *Blockälteste,* was a Christian Pole, and he could be just as cruel as a German. He had his own room in the barrack, separated from the rest of us.

Because there were so many long periods of inactivity, many of us dreamed about escaping. It was wishful thinking to believe we could ever accomplish this. Anyone who was caught trying to escape was brutally killed as an example to others. In most cases escape was deliberate suicide.

Even if one managed to get out of the immediate barracks area, there were electrified fences and mines to contend with. All of these fences and mine traps had been built by inmates and were so well constructed that they would have presented a challenge even for healthy men. Our rations were small, and we were run down, which meant that virtually none of us was up to trying to make a break for freedom. So we remained inside the barracks and, in order to survive, followed the strict rules as carefully as possible. Failing to remember even the smallest detail could be fatal.

Because there was no work, we were allowed to roam about the camp, and I used to go from barrack to barrack, meeting other inmates and getting more information about what was happening in the war. About a week after my arrival, I met a couple of men standing outside the entrance of a barrack and speaking in Russian. I talked with them and found out that they were part of a contingent of VIP Russian prisoners of war, a general, a colonel, a major, several captains, and a few lieutenants. The Nazis had separated them from the other prisoners with whom they had been captured. They were afraid that because of their high level of education, they were potential leaders. But instead of being incarcerated in a prisoner of war camp, they had been brought to Auschwitz. Several French government officials were also housed with them in the same barrack.

The Russians decided to introduce me to their leader and brought me inside to meet him. The general immediately sent them back outside to look for any SS. They were to knock on the wall in the event they saw any, and we would immediately get out, trying not to be observed. The general told us that the Germans were losing the war, that a Russian offensive had started, and that he was sure that if the West attacked in strength the war could be over later in 1944. I enjoyed talking with him and thought that we would have many more conversations about the war and just about life in general. But the next time I passed by that barrack there was a sign up at the entrance saying, "Entry Forbidden." I never saw them again, and I later heard that they had all been transferred to Dachau where they were shot.

# chapter 15

One day, several weeks after I had arrived in Auschwitz, an Oberscharführer came to the barrack and asked if there were any tailors present. A few of us stepped forward. He then brought out a pressing iron, scissors, thread, and needles. It was so important for him to look good that he promised to give us more food if we kept his clothes looking impeccable. He also gave us a sponge and a bottle of water to keep it moist. He told us, "Don't spit on the clothes, use the sponge instead!" He obviously was acquainted with the practice of the older generation of Polish tailors who used saliva to provide moisture when doing their ironing. That first day we repaired and pressed his clothes. Then the Oberscharführer introduced us to one SS officer after another, and we found ourselves tailoring all their clothes, still getting extra food in return.

Several weeks after we set up the "tailoring facility," the Blockälteste asked the inmates if any of us played chess. Since I could play fairly well, I stepped forward, along with a dozen or so others. The Blockälteste looked at each of us in the eye. "I am the Blockälteste," he said, "and you know I kill people. I want you to know that if you let me win just because you're afraid I'll kill you, then I really will do so. But if I see that you lost because you're not capable of beating me, then I'll give you some extra soup." His was not an idle threat. To maintain discipline in the barrack, he had been given the authority by the Germans to beat and to kill inmates, usually with the help of his two Gentile Polish assistants.

The chess games took place in the Blockälteste's office, a separate room that he occupied located in the barrack structure. For several days, everyone who played against him lost. Then it was my turn. After I sat down he said, "Before we start, I want you to understand one thing. You are to play your hardest. I want you to try your best to win. Don't appease me by letting me win without a fight!" So I played and I won. After the game he said, "Karl, in the future don't worry whether you win or not. You are someone I respect, and I won't hurt you." Then he gave me two extra bowls of soup.

This man still scared me. If I continued to win at chess he would become irritated and he might hurt and possibly kill me, to take his revenge. On the other hand, if I lost, he would know that I wasn't playing at my best, and the consequences could be equally disastrous.

I decided that the only way out was to side step the issue. The next time I was scheduled to play chess with him I diverted his attention by talking about clothes and suggesting to him that he would look much smarter if I fixed up his shabby looking outfit. Then, after he became eager for me to proceed with the tailoring, I truthfully said that I wasn't in the mood for chess that day, that maybe, instead, we should get to his clothes. He agreed, and I spent the next few hours working on his wardrobe.

My tailoring worked as a distraction only that one time; a few days later it was my turn again to play chess with him. This time, just as I was about to report to the Blockälteste's office to begin the game, the alarm whistles went off all over the camp. That meant that we all were supposed to run to the central part of our barrack and wait.

I positioned myself so I could look through the gap between the roof and the walls of the barrack to see what was happening. Before long, I saw German SS troops in full battle dress running towards the crematorium area. Then I heard fire engines heading in the same direction. I looked over to the crematorium and saw flames shooting up. There obviously was a fire, and it seemed to be out of control. But then the fire engines extinguished it, the alarm was turned off, the SS troops left, and things returned to normal. Fortunately, with all the tumult, there was no time for a chess game that day.

Three days later I found out what had happened. I had a friend who was a plumber. He was one of the few Jews who could travel all over the camp in order to make repairs. Of course, he was always escorted by an SS man, but he still was able to talk to other inmates, so that he could gather and relay information. He told me that he had talked to a crematorium worker and had found out that there had been a rebellion. Three of the workers had somehow obtained guns. They shot a guard, then took the hated three hundred pound German civilian who was in charge of crematorium operations, and threw him into the oven alive. Three of the rebels were caught. The others tried to escape, but very probably died in the process.

A few days later, early in the morning, while I was standing outside the barrack I noticed a man walking on the road with chains on his hands and legs. His head was swollen, and his face was cut and bleeding, he obviously had suffered terrible beatings. Two SS men were holding the ends of the chains, walking him in the direction of the SS headquarters. We later learned that this man, who was from Krakow, was the leader of the rebellion. They must have killed him soon afterwards.

Again, I started to worry about having to play another game of chess with the Blockälteste. I had been saved by the unsuccessful revolt, but I couldn't hope for any more lucky distractions. Fortunately for me, a few days later the Blockälteste found a distraction of his own and completely forgot about playing chess. Some Polish Christian women had been brought to Auschwitz and housed in a converted men's barrack nearby. When he found out about the new arrivals our Blockälteste immediately visited their barrack and began making friends. Then one night he brought over one of the women whom he had disguised in men's clothing. He ordered his two assistants to segregate part of our barrack with blankets and to make a comfortable place for the Blockälteste and the woman to sleep. After feeding her with salami and other good food, he slept with her the rest of the night.

The next night he brought in a different woman. He had become totally preoccupied with seducing the most attractive women of the group, and he never resumed his interest in playing chess while I remained at Auschwitz.

A few days after the revolt, I noticed German soldiers digging trenches, installing telephone and telegraph lines, and then covering the trenches with earth. I asked one inmate friend why they were doing all that excavating, and he said that they were making sure they had secure communications lines, in case they were forced to retreat.

One day in August of 1944, I noticed a new group of arrivals in Barrack 9, right next door. These were all Polish Christians, some one thousand of them. I talked to one of the men in that group and he told me that there had been an uprising of the Polish underground and that those captured had been sent to Auschwitz. He also told me that just before he had been arrested, the Germans had been slaughtering men, women, and children, and that his son, a medical intern working in a local hospital, had been killed by a German soldier for no apparent reason. The soldier had been waiting for the man's son in front of his house. When he arrived, dressed in his white uniform and wearing a red-cross armband, the soldier waited for him to walk into the doorway and then shot him.

At noon that day the Christian Poles were ordered to stand outside naked at attention for an inspection by Dr. Mengele. He went up and down the lines until he found one man who was circumcised. Mengele asked the man "Are you Jewish?"

"No, I'm not Jewish, I was born a Christian," the man said.

Mengele then started screaming, "confess, confess that you're a Jew!" When the man would not obey, Mengele started beating him with his fists until his face was bleeding. He then had the guards drag him away to what everyone was sure would be his death. One week later the rest of the group were all taken away and I never heard about them again. I am sure they were all gassed.

Our group of Poles was integrated with a number of Kalmuks, Asiatic Russians, who had been captured by the Germans during the war. The Kalmuks had small noses and eyes. Some of them were loyal to the Germans. Others had fought for the Russians. This particular group had served the Nazis as mounted troops and had fought the Russians, but they somehow had fallen out of favor and been dumped in with the Jews. Personally, I didn't like to be around them. I knew that they had been used by the Nazis to find and kill Jews who were hiding in the countryside. They had been outfitted with horses and weapons and had roamed the fields killing any partisans and Jews they could find.

One day the Blockälteste ordered his Polish Christian subordinates to attack the Kalmuks, and they beat them severely with wooden two-by-fours. The next day, one Kalmuk who was an officer and who spoke German fluently told the SS that the Poles had beaten them. The SS punished the Blockälteste by whipping him with fifteen lashes while he was bent over a bench.

Shortly afterwards a Russian inmate reminded the Germans that the war might be going against them. "You're losing the war. You'd better be careful how you treat us," he said. Then the Russian tried to seize the guard's pistol. Other German guards arrived quickly and a shooting was avoided only after some of the Nazis warned the others that they "did not have the right" to execute Russians. Up until that time I hadn't noticed any differences in how prisoners were treated, but now I was aware that there were some differences between prisoner classes. The guards could do anything they wanted with us Jews, but when it came to non-Jewish inmates, such as the Russians or the Kalmuks, they had to be a little more careful.

# chapter 16

In our barrack was a small, oven-style, brick furnace. It was about forty inches long and was built in a rectangle with a half-rounded shape top which could be opened. If we had coal, the oven could have given us heat. But there wasn't any, and I soon learned that the oven was put to another use.

If an inmate rose in the night to relieve himself, he risked not being able to find a place to sleep when he returned. Those who were sleeping were packed so tightly on the ledges that, by the time he got back, all the others on his shelf might have redistributed themselves so that his space was gone.

Two Christian Poles were on duty all night. They worked under the Block-älteste. If anyone took longer than ten minutes to squeeze back into the pack of bodies on the sleeping shelf, these kapos would pull him aside and take him to this barrack oven, which we had nicknamed "the Guillotine." The Poles would place the inmate's head in the oven with his body spread over a locker. An iron bar was mounted right over the opening of the oven so that it could be locked over the back of the man's head making it impossible to get out. With a piece of hardwood, a guard would hit the man in the lower back in such a way as to damage or possibly break his spine. Then the inmate would be released from the oven, laid out on his back and killed by "grand chucking," another favorite method that the Blockältestes and their Polish assistants used to kill Jews.

To "grand chuck," the Poles would throw the victim on the ground. Then a heavy piece of wood was placed across the victim's neck and one of the Poles would exert pressure on the plank by rocking back and forth. The victim was usually dead within a few minutes. I was more afraid of "grand chucking" than of the gas chamber.

One night we saw some prisoners piling up bodies outside the crematorium, as if the corpses were sticks of firewood. Later we learned that the number of arrivals had increased and the crematorium could not keep up with the load. The ovens could burn the bodies in a relatively short period of time, but the gas chambers could easily surpass them in volume.

Near the crematorium was an area blocked out by brown military blankets suspended some seven feet off the ground. After a while, I became curious about the large number of SS men who kept visiting the place. They were armed and dressed as if they going to a full-dress parade. It turned out that behind the blanket fence the Germans had assigned inmates to inspect the bodies of the dead, searching for valuables before they were cremated. They cut the long hair of the women, pulled gold teeth from mouths, and searched body orifices for hidden jewelry and valuables. The SS supervised this morbid work.

In the same manner that we had been introduced to the camp, people headed for the gas chambers would be told that they were going to the showers and that they should undress. The Germans also insisted that any valuables being carried be placed in a large barrel, but they didn't search each person carefully before he or she entered the gas chambers. Thus, despite the Nazis' best efforts, many prisoners went to their deaths wearing small items of jewelry like rings or earrings. Sometimes prisoners had managed to hide such valuables; sometimes the killing went on at such a rapid rate that there was no time to search the living.

Even though we were completely dominated by the Germans, many among us were not entirely submissive. I heard about one young Jewish woman from Warsaw, who soon after she arrived at the camp, refused to remove her brassiere when asked to undress.

An SS man approached her with a gun and attempted to force her to remove the garment. She hit the man in the face with the brassiere, took his gun away, and shot him in the face. Her courage gave many others strength, even though she was killed for her actions.

As people were being forced to enter the chambers that would soon be filled with the Zyklon-B poison gas, they could smell the residual odor in the area just outside the chambers. By that time many knew that they were going to be killed. We could hear their voices calling out, "God, my God." Some of the people called out in Hebrew, "Hear oh Israel, the Lord our God, the Lord is one." With those few brief words, they prepared to die.

After being gassed, their bodies had to be removed from the gas chambers. The inmates doing the stacking were Jewish, but they seemed to be a little insane, perhaps due to the nature of the gruesome tasks they were performing. One group, using large iron forks and pincers, pulled and dragged out the bodies from the gas chambers, while another searched them for gold teeth and other valuables. Once stripped, the bodies were stacked like so many logs, men, women, and children together, waiting to be placed in the ovens.

We saw the smoke and the flames, and we felt the heat and breathed the air laden with that terrible burning flesh odor. There was no choice but to breathe it. We lived with the knowledge that what was happening to others would soon probably happen to us.

Though the number of people killed each day was very large, there remained some ten thousand people in the camp. There were eleven major barracks and each housed eight or nine hundred people. Although rations were small, very few of us starved. Many, however, died from sickness.

◆ ◆ ◆

Late one night the guards came into the barrack and ordered us out into the night. All around the camp there were large billboards covered with slogans and threats. That night all the billboards were lighted. Some of the signs said that there was no God. Others said, "We are the rulers, there is no God here, so don't look for help."

We lined up in the dark and soon I became aware of the shadowy images of four men in front of us. It was hard to see them in the dark, but I realized that they were inmates. They wore striped uniforms and held shovels, and they didn't move. Suddenly SS men turned bright lights on the four men. Their faces had been touched up with cosmetics, and they seemed to be propped up against wooden boards, like mannequins. An SS man stood in front of us and said, "All of you look straight ahead and do not let your eyes drop to the ground. I will be watching you and if any of you fail to follow my order, you will be standing over there with those four men."

The SS man continued his speech. "Look at that man," he said, pointing to the one nearest him. "Take it all into your mind. This is a warning that you should understand. These men have been lazy, they did not want to perform the work we ordered them to do. They cheated on the orders to finish certain tasks. You are warned that you must follow orders and then your willingness will be rewarded." He continued on that theme for a few minutes, and we just stood there, wondering what was going to happen next. When the SS man finished his exhortation, he walked over to the men and kicked away the supporting boards. They collapsed in a heap. They weren't mannequins. They were human corpses.

The SS man said, "They were killed because they didn't work well at our bidding. Be sure to keep a picture of them in your mind. If you do not do what we want, then you too will be here tomorrow for the same punishment."

◆ ◆ ◆

Like so many other things at Auschwitz and the other camps, even the simplest of our activities was meant to be demeaning. Food for ten people was placed on one bowl. The ten of us were expected to take turns eating. Usually there wasn't much left for the last person.

Every morning we were awakened by the Blockälteste before sunrise. Then, even during the coldest weather, we were required to stand outside until ten A.M., waiting for an inspection and headcount. Anyone who was sick or who reported having a headache was taken to the first aid station. Usually they never returned. If they did, a truck might come for them later. The driver had a list of those inmates who were to be gassed, and there was no place for those selected to hide. They were driven directly to the gas chambers. All of them knew they were going on their last ride. Several told the rest of us, who remained, that when they died and went to heaven they would ask why Jews had been singled out for torture and annihilation. This was a question all of us wondered about and for which we had no answer.

Headaches and dizziness were common, particularly the day after a beating. These were a daily routine. I was hit several times with two-by-fours, bamboo sticks, and canes. It was important not to let the Blockälteste know if you were feeling sick or injured. A rule of thumb for survival was to avoid the first aid station at all costs.

In the summer we had a special problem with sanitation. We were only allowed to use the latrines during the day. In June and July the toilet seats were covered with maggots and were white with the creatures. If you expected a bowel movement there was no choice but to brush the maggots aside and sit down. Certain inmates were assigned to the duty of watching the "performers" to make sure everyone sat down. If you refused, you could be beaten and thrown into the pile of human feces. If the maggots managed to bite, you had a good chance of getting an infection. Almost all of us became infected, and, as a result, suffered from a terrible swelling of the genitals. The pain was often so acute that men begged to die. There were several young boys, only twelve years old, who also suffered terribly from this.

One very warm evening we were ordered to line up. The infection was so painful that it was difficult for me to walk or to stand for more than a few minutes. Dr. Mengele, who was present, ordered those of us who were sick to line up for a special inspection. I thought that then would be my death sentence. Surely all of us who were ill would be dead soon. Much to our surprise and relief, Mengele ordered us to stay out in the sun all day. A few hours after his first inspection, we were given an ointment which we applied to the infected areas. Within hours we began to have some relief, and after three days, we were back to normal.

Mengele was the same man who was responsible for all kinds of heinous acts, yet his generosity at that time kept us alive. We knew that he could have sent us to the gas chambers just as easily as he had helped us. Fortunately, the incident occurred at a time when we sorely needed something to bolster our hopes of somehow surviving Auschwitz and the war.

As terrifying to us as the gas chambers, was the threat of becoming victims of medical experiments. Every day throughout the summer of 1944 the guards would call men from my barrack and take them to a first aid station where medical experiments were being conducted. Three or four hours later, they would return, screaming and crying, in terrible pain.

I saw one man who returned from the first aid station with the skin on his belly cut open and then rolled back to the middle of his rib cage. He was in agony and couldn't stop screaming. The Germans had applied some substance on the raw wounds and then repositioned the skin, stitching it back into place. When I asked him what they had done, he opened his shirt and showed me the large area where they had cut him open; I could see all the stitches. He was a guinea pig for the Germans to practice on while learning how to treat wounds. Another healthy man was taken from the barrack one day and returned castrated. This was a daily occurrence.

I remember the day that a young twenty-four-year-old man, who was the son of a rabbi from Radom and who was a highly educated, Orthodox Jew, was taken to the first aid station for a medical experiment. They burned his skin black and when he came back, he was in terrible pain. I remember that, between his screams, he said, "My dear brothers of the faith of Moses, my week of experiences makes me want to die." He had been given a card, which stated that he was going to be taken to the gas chamber. He said, "I am going to die as an offering, because the Jews believe that there is life after death." The young man assured us that he was planning to "talk to the judge of judges, the high tribunal above" and told us that he would pray and ask God to help us survive the Holocaust. A few hours later a truck arrived and took him to the gas chamber.

◆ ◆ ◆

Besides us Jews there were also a small number of Gentile inmates. They were often assigned to special work projects; construction and repair of railroad tracks, working in nearby chemical plants, and other jobs outside the camp.

The women were segregated from the men and lived in the same kind of barracks. Some of these were only twenty feet apart and were separated by a high voltage, electrified fence. I was able to talk to women inmates by standing close to one of these fences. I heard that some of the women had been taken to a bordello located in Auschwitz. There was a policy in Auschwitz that applied only to male Christian inmates who worked for the Germans as supervisors and were called kapos. Whenever one of them did a particularly good job he would be rewarded with a coupon that would entitle him to have sexual relations with a woman in the bordello. There were also rumors that pregnancy experiments were conducted in the camp. All victims of medical experiments, both men and women, were virtually assured of death as soon as the experiments were finished.

◆ ◆ ◆

One day about two hundred and 25 or 50 young men came to Auschwitz and were brought into the barracks. Some were only nine years old, the oldest was about thirteen. A number were Lithuanian Jews from the ghetto at Vilna and the others were from Jewish areas on the Baltic. They had been in Dachau, but the commandant there didn't want them because they were too young and small for hard work. So he sent them off to Auschwitz to be exterminated.

Those young men brought the first real news we had about all of our countrymen and their trials and tribulations. We learned of the destruction of the Warsaw ghetto. In the four weeks that they were with us, we could see that they were very bright and well educated. Some could speak four or five languages, including Russian, Hebrew, Yiddish, German, and in a few cases, French. Many were the children of professionals—doctors, engineers, and others.

I had many conversations with them and found that they were generally wise beyond their years. Those young men were able to discuss questions of life and death with unusual maturity. They understood why they were being held as prisoners, and they were aware that their lives were in peril. We had long discussions about our faith and what it meant to be a Jew. The conversations always seemed to center around the "punishment" we were receiving because we were Jews.

Then one day they were all called outside, loaded into a truck, and taken to the gas chambers. They may have been cremated that very night because a few hours after they were taken, the chimneys began to belch smoke. Two of the young men managed to hide out in the barrack, and they survived. I know they did because after I was liberated, I saw one of them in Germany with his father.

The Blockälteste of our barrack saw them and, instead of turning them over to the Germans, decided to keep them alive. He was able to hide their presence by counting them as part of another group which arrived shortly after the young men had been taken away. Integrated with another group of inmates, they were never detected by the Germans.

◆ ◆ ◆

While at the time we never really considered ourselves as heroic, we saw many examples of heroism and self sacrifice. There were two brothers from Radom who were fourteen and twenty-two years old and who had been with me in Blizyn. After one of the frequent inspections, Mengele ordered that some twenty-five of the youngest men in the barrack, including the younger brother of these two, be given white bread, margarine, and a cup of milk with sugar. This was very unusual treatment in the camp.

The younger boy gave his portion of food to his older brother, observing that he knew that he had been given the food because the group was going to die. Perhaps the food would enable his brother to live a little longer. His assumption was correct. Shortly after the food had been distributed, the SS came and herded the twenty-five young men out into the night and loaded them onto trucks. They may have abused them first, but we were certain they ended up in the gas chambers.

One night, at midnight in late August of 1944, we were abruptly awakened by bright lights in our barrack and blaring loudspeakers. All eight hundred of us were ordered outside and told to line up into formation immediately. It happened very quickly and we reacted partly from habit. In a few moments we formed in six lines and were told we were going to take showers. We started marching toward them—the direction of the gas chambers and crematorium. The whole area was bright with search lights. It was an eerie sight. Certain parts of the camp were separated from others by electrified, barbed-wire fences. The showers and gas chambers were behind such a fence which was monitored by guards carrying rifles with fixed bayonets. They used the bayonets to prod us as we marched along. They also beat some of us with night sticks. The Ukrainians were those murderous SS men in German uniforms who used their bayonets to wound us.

The march was slow. In about half-an-hour we came almost to a standstill. We knew that we were walking toward death. We had seen neighboring barracks emptied in the middle of the night and we never saw any of their inmates again.

All in our group were Jews. Many were praying and using their right hands to beat their chests, asking God's forgiveness in the manner of a priest or rabbi intoning the last prayers for someone about to die. We were sure that these prayers would be our last. Most of the people were chanting: "He being merciful, forgive iniquity and destroy not yet. Many a time he turned his anger away and did not stir up all his wrath." I chose another one which begged God to shorten the span of my life and give me a quick death. I accepted my fate of the gas chamber and prayed that it would be as painless as possible. I thought about what it would be like walking into the gas chamber. I imagined that when I entered I would be able to taste the poisonous Zyklon-B, and that by inhaling deeply I would experience the sweet death that would end my human suffering.

A Red Cross ambulance was parked in the area as we approached. It was routine for the SS to transport the pellets which produced the gas in Red Cross trucks. Maybe they were meant to serve as decoys for the Allied airplanes which sometimes flew over the camp. As we learned recently, it was an unnecessary precaution. Even though the British and American planes took pictures of Auschwitz while I was there, the Allies could not understand what the pictures showed.

As we marched, I thought about death and continued to pray for a quick end to my life. I prayed, "God, dear God. You created me and I know that the span of life can be sixty, seventy, eighty, or ninety years, and I now feel as if I were one hundred years old. I am leaving this world." It was easy marching after that. As we drew closer to the gas chambers, we noticed two very large German shepherd dogs on the outside of the line snapping at and biting the prisoners. There were also two huge searchlights, and they were focused on the entrance to the chambers and crematoriums. The ovens were located in a wooded area nearby. The night would have been very dark without those lights.

Then, almost like a scene out of a movie, we saw two motorcycles approaching in the darkness. They were driving very fast as they approached the electrified gate to the area where we were being held. The guards opened the gate for the two riders. We couldn't do a lot of looking around, but I did notice that the riders were SS men, armed with lightweight machine guns and in full battle dress. They loudly demanded to see the commander in charge of the group. The guards told them that he was at the entrance to the gas chamber and couldn't be disturbed. Ten minutes later, the camp officer finally appeared. He was an SS Obersturmbannführer, a higher rank than a colonel. The men got off their motorcycles, gave him a *"Heil Hitler!"* salute and handed him a large envelope. In German they said, "Obersturmbannführer, here is an order from Berlin from the Labor Department. This group of people is to be held here to be available for transport to labor camps in Germany."

Just minutes before, the officer in charge was to have sent the first of our group into the gas chambers, our reprieve came. The order not to kill us was almost too late. It was unusual to have gone to so much trouble to spare us. Perhaps they really needed workers. Like so many things about the whole Nazi regime, there was no rhyme or reason. They were in command and could do as they pleased. It just happened that it pleased them to spare us at that particular time.

The camp's Obersturmbannführer was furious when he heard the news. He looked like a wild beast as he called us "shit" and fumed. I can never forget the rage in his face. The two couriers asked him to sign a receipt stating that he had received the orders and would carry them out. The Obersturmbannführer shouted, "Shit, turn around." We marched back to the barracks from which we had left earlier that night. Even those who were wounded by the beatings and those who had been bitten by the dogs were allowed to return.

In September I was moved from the quarantine barrack to "C Lager," which was also known as the "Gypsy Camp" because of the large number of them who were kept there. There were five hundred men in my barrack. The Germans who were in charge were convicted sexual offenders and homosexuals who took delight in having the inmates participate in their brand of "fun."

One night the Blockälteste told us they were going to have a party. He gave us some greasy black shoe polish and told us to smear it over our faces so we would look like minstrels. Next, we had to take off all our clothes. Then we were ordered to tear some sheets into long, narrow pieces of cloth. The German in charge told us to tie the end of one of these strips onto our penises and the other to another inmate's penis so that eventually we all would be connected to each other in one long line. When that was done we were told to dance around and act like wild animals, while the Germans simply watched, laughing and obviously taking pleasure from the "circus" they were witnessing. After the performance was over they left us alone. It was one of the strangest nights of my life.

◆◆◆

My mother, father, my sister, Toba, and my brother, Nathan David, had all been at Blizyn where I saw them frequently. Then, my father was transported from Blizyn to a slave labor camp. Shortly afterwards, when we were moved to Auschwitz, Toba was sent to work outside the camp, and Nathan David and I were separated from our mother. In all the time I was in Auschwitz I had not seen my mother until one very chilly, icy fall morning, around the time of Yom Kippur, when I saw a group of some five hundred naked women being forced to do gymnastic exercises. The SS women in charge were forcing them to crawl on their hands and knees on a pathway of very sharp gravel. Each woman's head had been shaved, either as a punishment or because the Germans had a use for their hair. After crawling on the gravel, they were forced to run. While they were doing this, I recognized my mother among the group. Until that time I wasn't sure whether my mother had survived the initial selection process. I tried signaling by waving my hand. She must have seen me because at lunch time she walked close to the fence to talk with me. The barbed wire separated us, but it was good to see and talk with her. She told me that Nathan David was working as a transport kommando and had been throwing bread over a fence for herself and her cousin Rachel. If I came to the same spot the next day Rachel would throw some of the bread to me. Then she said goodbye. We were lucky. None of the guards had seen us.

The next day I found Rachel near the place where I had seen my mother. She didn't say anything but threw a piece of bread over the fence so strongly that I had to run to catch it. I didn't stop running until I reached the safety of my barrack.

Three days later, at the same area, I saw mother waving to me. I went over to the barbed-wire fence and, just as we began to talk, an SS guard noticed us and ran over to me. As he screamed, he took a wooden cane and started beating and kicking me at the same time. Then he noticed another man talking to a woman across the barbed wire. He left me and headed towards him, and since he wasn't looking I was able to crawl over to my barrack, where I hid under one of the bunks. A few minutes later the guard entered the barrack and shouted, "Come out," but I didn't make a sound. I suppose he thought I might have gone somewhere else because he stormed off.

My legs were severely injured, and I couldn't walk for days. Because we were in the quarantine barrack where I had no work assignment, I was able to recuperate without being noticed. The beating left me with permanent scars and with irreparably damaged blood vessels in my legs.

A few weeks later, just before Rosh Hashonah, I met my mother again at the same place. We were careful not to talk until we were sure that no one was watching. Then my mother told me the news. Nathan David had stopped showing up to throw bread to Rachel, and she was convinced that he was no longer with the transport kommandos. She said, "My son Kiwa, I hope that all three of my children will survive. But I know that father and I will never survive." She pointed toward the smoke coming out of the crematorium chimney and told me that she was certain that she would die that way.

I said, "No, don't live to die. Be strong enough to live with hope. Don't think of dying. The Russian army is coming and the Germans are losing the war." But she was still pessimistic. She said, "My last wish is that some or all of my children should survive. But if you do, take revenge on the Germans, tell the story." She blessed me and we said goodbye.

◆ ◆ ◆

The day before Yom Kippur in 1944 nearly all of the Jews in our part of the camp agreed that we would fast and pray during the holiday. At five o'clock in the morning, just before daybreak, the guards ordered us out of the barracks and told us to line up in formation, facing north. They told us to take off our striped uniforms and wait, naked, in line. It was cold, and we were all shivering. At eight in the morning the Blockälteste announced that Mengele was coming over to make a selection. We waited another two hours. Then, sometime around ten in the morning, Mengele arrived in full dress uniform, along with two high-ranking and five lower ranked SS officers.

Mengele stood in front of us and very solemnly said, *"Ich bin der Gott von Leben und Tod"* ("I am the God over life and death."). Then he and his entourage walked up and down each line. He selected some of us and passed others by. It wasn't clear why he chose the ones he did, but he seemed to pick every eighth or ninth man, until he had selected some four hundred from our group. He chose men on either side of me, but he somehow did not pick me. When he was finished, he said, "You know you are Jews, and as it is traditional, God needs offerings, just as it was done in the early days in the temple. Today it is Yom Kippur eve and tomorrow will be your Day of Atonement. Some of you will have to go as offerings, because the Jewish God needs them."

Mengele then made one more pass walking down the lines of those who remained unchosen. Every so often he would stand in front of a man and ask him to look into his eyes. If he saw any hesitation, if the man's eyes moved or if the man trembled, Mengele had him removed from the line. That meant the man was "selected." Mengele picked one young man to my immediate right and passed on to the end of the line. At that point I thought I had made it through this selection, but just then he turned around and came back again, this time picking the man on my immediate left. Then he stood directly in front of me, asking me to look into his eyes. I stood still as a statue as I looked directly into his eyes and he looked into mine. It was eerie. It was as if he was trying to read my mind, to discover the secrets of my soul. I knew that if I thought about the situation I would become nervous and flinch. That meant death. So I adopted a mental arrogance. I decided to turn the tables on him and try to explore his "soul" as I gazed intensely into his eyes. I probed and he probed and all I came up with was nothing. I tried harder, looking for clues, for something to explain why this monster of a man did what he did. And then, in an instant, Mengele moved on, leaving me standing in the line of men destined to be survivors of this selection. Mengele pointed to the group of several hundred men he had selected. "These men will leave Auschwitz through the chimneys," he said. "You watch them become an offering for you and be thankful." Then he ordered us to return to our barracks.

The men Mengele had selected were inventoried by the numbers tattooed on their arms. Just after noon the guards began calling out their numbers, and one by one they left the barracks and boarded the trucks that stood outside waiting for them. They were taken to the gas chambers.

After the men had been taken away, the survivors got together to observe Yom Kippur. We began to organize at midday, and by nightfall everything was ready. One member of our group, a very religious man named Holewa, was a cantor from Czenstochowa, Poland, a city known for its holy men, even though it was primarily a Christian city. He agreed to conduct a Kol Nidre service with prayers that evening.

Everyone agreed to fast. Our unity helped convince the Blockälteste that we were serious about our observance so he overlooked our activities. Although it was risky, we all saved the rations from the daytime meal on Yom Kippur. We didn't eat the soup, and we saved our bread and even avoided drinking any water all that day.

Holewa was prepared to lead the service from memory. He had a wonderful voice. The SS men in charge of Blizyn had tried to get Holewa to sing arias, he told us that he would rather die than provide entertainment for the Nazis. We had told the Nazis there that he could sing only the Hebrew prayers and that he didn't know the arias they wanted to hear.

At six o'clock, with the permission of the Christian Blockälteste and his helpers, we began our observance. They risked breaking the rules to let us have the service. Hazan Holewa began the service with his beautiful voice, and our eyes filled with tears. The Blockälteste came closer and soon he too was crying. One of the Jewish plumbers in our camp had managed to smuggle in a prayer book by tying it against his body as he entered the camp. It was the only reference we had. We conducted the rest of the service from memory.

All day long we fasted and prayed. Even some of the young Russian atheists from our barrack participated, although they didn't pray. Crying and lamenting, we prayed to God, the King of Kings, begging for redemption and release from our suffering. Holewa said at one point, "I pray for you, God, King of Kings, and I pray for all your children as they are here." With his prayer, he offered himself as a sacrifice, so that the rest of us would not die at the hands of the Nazis.

It chilled me to the bone that this man would cry out to God, asking that we be saved by his sacrifice. We were praying to God who had not interceded for all those who had gone before us into the gas chambers, or who had died before the firing squads or beneath the blows of the guards or the torture of the medical "experiments." We were praying from Auschwitz for the miracle that all those others had prayed for, too. Even when the very idea of surviving could drive a person to the brink of madness, we prayed to survive.

The Blockälteste stood up as the stars appeared in the evening sky. It was time to finish the service, although we continued to fast into the next day. The Block-älteste said that he felt we had suffered enough and had perhaps caused ourselves some unnecessary anxiety by dwelling on the subject of survival. He told us he thought that some of us would survive. Then he said it was time to break up the assemblage because the SS would soon be coming to check the barracks.

We lay down and feigned sleep until the guards completed their rounds. Then we began to pray again. Finally, when we had finished and the fasting was over, we ate the bread and soup we had saved. To have fasted and prayed in Auschwitz may seem incomprehensible, but at the time, it allowed us to believe that there was still hope, that the Nazis had not completely broken our spirits.

# chapter 18

A few days later, at night, the food rations were discontinued. Now, we thought, we would surely be sent to the gas chambers — or that the Germans would starve us to death. It was a false alarm. Two days later we were given food once again.

Generally, the Gypsies in the nearby barracks had more freedom than we had and made lots of noise as they moved around. A few days after the starvation scare, very late at night, we heard trucks moving, and people being wakened and herded outdoors. Then it became very quiet. The rest of that night and during the next day no sounds came from the Gypsy barracks. They had been taken away to the gas chambers. This was at the end of October 1944.

Not long after the Gypsies disappeared, we were rousted out of our barracks for yet another "shower." This time we were herded toward an area which was not near the chimneys so we knew we were safe. After the shower we were issued new striped uniforms and taken to a cattle loading ramp at the stockyards in the Auschwitz rail station. As we boarded the cattle cars we were each given some bread. Then the doors to the cattle cars were locked, and the train pulled away from Auschwitz.

Inside, we were packed so tightly that each person had to intertwine his legs with another to provide enough room to sit on the floor. There was a bucket of water in the car but no food apart from the bread we had been given. We had no idea where we were being taken. All we knew was that we were alive, and that we were out of that terrible place. What a miracle it was that we had survived.

◆ ◆ ◆

There must have been almost five thousand Jews in the train. In the car with me was a group of some two hundred Sephardic Jews, some from North Africa who had been brought to Auschwitz towards the end of July, others from the Greek island of Rhodes. They were all healthy, tanned, well educated, and wealthy. They didn't speak Yiddish at all, but Hebrew, Italian, French, and Arabic. By talking with them in Hebrew we learned that they had been evacuated by airplane, some just before the Allies were about to liberate the places where they had lived.

These Sephardim hadn't fared too well at Auschwitz. They had quickly become depressed and many simply lost the will to live. They began to die both by committing suicide and for no apparent reason other than "heartbreak." Now we were in the train and those who were left were being squeezed into the cattle car along with the European Jews. But unlike the rest of us who were already used to the crowded, unhealthy conditions, these "newcomers" from a different world couldn't stand the odors, the tightness, the torture of being packed like sardines, and they began to die. During that first day in the train only a few of them died, but many more would do so before our journey was over.

From Auschwitz, the train took us to the central station in Vienna. There, SS men opened the doors and gave us some more water and a ration of bread. We piled the bodies of those who had died en route at one end of the car to give the rest of us some extra space. There were, of course, no toilet facilities in the cattle cars, and the odor of urine and excrement soon replaced the searing flesh odor we had learned to live with at Auschwitz.

We stopped in Vienna for only a few hours. Then the doors were closed again and the train started to move, this time towards Linz. We changed locomotives at Salzburg, apparently to help make the climb up the rugged terrain. From Salzburg we proceeded towards Munich. Once again, we charted our course by watching the signs along the way.

After the train left Vienna, more and more of the Sephardim died until only a few of the original group of two hundred were still alive. We continued to pile the bodies on top of each other, all the way up to the ceiling of the railroad car. For those who survived there now was more room to move about.

The train arrived at Munich where it waited on a siding. German guards told us that we would either be going to a camp called "Dachau," which was located nearby, or we would be taken to Kaufering, a subsidiary camp of Dachau, approximately eighty miles to the north. After a while the train started moving north, and we knew we were headed for Kaufering.

It was about midnight when we arrived, and we had no idea what was going to happen to us. We had been taken from one camp which had been an extermination center only to land in another one, the nature of which remained unknown.

As we were unloaded from the cattle cars we saw lots of SS men talking in loud voices. Some of them wore the insignia of the rank of Oberscharführer, the highest-ranking sergeant, and at least one of them was an SS *Sturmbannführer*. They carried rubber sticks in their hands, and they ordered us to leave the train in a bizarre manner: to jump and land in a squat position. Those who lost their balance or failed to land on their feet were beaten on their heads and shoulders with the rubber nightsticks. The SS men kept yelling, "You are condemned Jews, pigs—jump down, you are going to die here." I managed to land on my feet and avoided a severe beating.

After I passed the first line of SS men—those who were beating my fellow prisoners as we jumped—I discovered another group waiting to line us up into military formations. We were separated into groups of approximately one hundred each and then were marched from the rail station to the camp. We marched for two hours, and I was surprised to discover that, despite the beatings at the station, the guards here seemed less brutal than those at Auschwitz. We asked them what was going to happen to us, and they began to tell us what Kaufering was all about.

Apparently, there were some thirty thousand Jews in eleven camps at Kaufering. Most of them were from the Baltics, especially Latvia and Lithuania. I was taken to camp seven as part of a contingent of about three thousand Jews; there I was assigned to a barrack occupied mostly by people from the Baltic countries. The first question we new arrivals asked was, were there any crematoriums in the camp? The *Lagerkapo*, a German criminal who was assigned to supervise us, told us there were none. We then asked for some water, since the water on the train was used up long before our arrival and we were terribly thirsty. When we were given water I drank about two liters. Later that night we learned more about the camp from some of the other inmates. They confirmed what the guard had told us: there were no crematoriums.

My barrack at Kaufering was different from those at Blizyn or Auschwitz—not so much a building as a roof over a hole in the ground with five steps down to the lowest level. There was one tiny window in the roof and one electric lightbulb. There was almost no room in which to move around, and the sleeping facilities were wooden boards covered with dirty straw.

The next morning they put us to work. On the way we saw the train which had brought us being loaded with sick Baltic Jews. There were about two thousand of them, and they probably were headed back to Auschwitz. Many could hardly walk. At Auschwitz the health of a prisoner didn't really matter; inmates who got sick were just taken to the gas chambers. At Kaufering, however, there was no easy way to dispose of large numbers of sick prisoners. I realized that we had merely been exchanged—healthy Jews for sick, exhausted ones. It was also clear that after we had been drained of our strength and health, we, too, would be given a return trip back to the gas chambers.

In some ways discipline at Kaufering was more lenient than at Auschwitz; in other ways it was stricter. The food was inedible, and more attention was paid to enforcing the elaborate rules of the camp. Any minor violation, such as an inmate taking a piece of cloth to use as a handkerchief, was punishable by hanging. It was November of 1944, and it was very cold as we prayed that we might live through the rest of the year.

This was a particularly severe autumn, very cold and with frequent heavy rains. The Kaufering camp was surrounded by a forest, dense and when it rained, everything turned to mud. The ankle-deep mud caused serious problems. Sometimes, inmates who were trying to find their way to the only latrine in the camp were so weak that they couldn't pull their feet from the slippery ground without throwing themselves off balance. They would then fall face-down into the mud.

It got so bad that bulldozers were brought in to dig drainage ditches. The ditches weren't very wide, and a man in good health could easily have jumped over them, but for those of us who were weak it was impossible. So a board was placed across any ditch that required fording. Every day one or two inmates were found dead, lying in the ditches. They had fallen from a plank and couldn't rise. Some may have tried to jump across, while others had probably tried to walk the plank and had lost their balance, fallen, and drowned. It was a pitiful way to die.

The mud caused other problems, too. It was not uncommon for prisoners to get their feet caught in the mire and have a difficult time pulling them out. Many inmates lost their shoes trying to get their feet out. Shoes were very important for survival because of the constant danger of pneumonia. Some of the inmates still had leather shoes, but many wore only wooden clogs. If one's shoes wore out or fell apart, as they frequently did because of the heavy work and the bad weather, it was a virtual death sentence. He was not given a replacement pair, and it was only a matter of time before his feet would be injured or infected or he would develop pneumonia. Not that shoes were in short supply. With all the deaths there were plenty in the camp storehouse, and, also, the Blockältestes and the foremen of work parties were always able to find good shoes for themselves. Sometimes, in fact, if they found that an inmate had good shoes, they would take them and give him a pair of wooden clogs as a one-time replacement.

One morning when it was time for the work call, I found that the thin leather soles of my shoes had rotted through. I did what I could, fabricating cardboard substitute soles and using wire and old cement bags to keep them in place, but I knew that it would only take a day or two of walking in the mud before the condition of my feet would not permit me to work.

That day we weren't required to make the usual long march in the wet dirt to work, so I had at least a one day reprieve. The guards handling the work detail told us we were being "given the opportunity to volunteer for some special jobs." Under the usual conditions, volunteering meant that there was hard work and possibly a beating in store. For some reason the German kapos were screaming, "It is in your very best interests to volunteer." They were hinting that we might be beaten if we didn't. So rather than risk another beating, I volunteered and was selected to be one of sixteen for the special detail.

We were sent to an SS barrack that had its own kitchen, laundry room, offices, and living quarters. Our work was to set some new clothesline poles up behind the barrack. Many of the men who had volunteered, particularly the Hungarian Jews who were among the most recent shipment from Budapest, were in no shape for hard labor. They just lacked the strength to push the shovels into the ground. Because I was still strong, I took on more than my fair share of the tasks.

As we worked, a Wehrmacht officer—an *Oberfeldfabel,* or warrant officer—was watching us from a window. After a while, he came out of the building with his adjutant and approached our work detail. By now, we had all learned to snap to attention whenever a German officer approached. We stopped what we were doing and stood as straight and as tall as we possibly could. The officer came over to me and asked me where I had learned to dig holes so well.

"In the Polish army," I replied. "And what is your profession," he asked. "I'm a tailor."

"All right," he said. "I'm going to try you out as a tailor, and if you're not really one you will be whipped for lying."

The Oberfeldfabel told his adjutant to take me inside to a washroom. I felt very strange. Here I was, filthy and covered with lice, and still wearing the same clothes I had been given when I left Auschwitz. The adjutant ordered clean clothes for me: underwear, a shirt, and socks. I decided to be bold. "Sir, can you get me a new pair of shoes?"

The adjutant was a man of about sixty, named Tobias. He was surprised that I understood the German insignia of rank and asked me where I had learned about it. I told him of my experiences at Wolanow working for Otto Busse at the air base. He added shoes to the requisition order, and, along with the clean clothes and shoes, he gave me a razor and some soap. Then he left, after assigning a soldier to watch me and retrieve the razor when I had finished.

It had been a long time since I bathed in hot water. My body had become home for thousands of lice and some of them were not about to be dislodged by mere hot water and soap. I had to squeeze out the lice with my fingers. It was such a good feeling to be clean after having lived in filth for so long that I felt like a new man. I began to hope again. I felt as if a miracle had happened.

It was lunchtime when I finished cleaning myself. Tobias returned and asked me if I was hungry. I didn't want to appear greedy so I just said, "I could use a bite of bread." Tobias suddenly realized that we had been talking in German the whole time. He asked me how I had learned the language so well. I told him that I had learned as a child and used it on a daily basis when I lived in Wolanow. When I stopped to think about it, I realized that I had spoken German a great deal since the Polish army had surrendered outside Warsaw.

The Oberfeldfabel had also told Tobias to bring soup, bread, margarine, and other leftovers from the SS kitchen. While the soup didn't have any meat in it, it did have plenty of noodles. There is no way to describe the feelings of being "worthwhile" that began to infiltrate into my brain. I was actually feeling good about being alive. It was the best meal I had eaten since I became an inmate.

After lunch Tobias said there was work to be done. The Oberfeldfabel's uniform needed some new braid sewn onto it. After searching, one of Tobias' subordinates found a needle, a thimble, and scissors. Then, in a lighted corner of the washroom, I went to work. One of the subordinates whispered, "If you are not a tailor and do not know how to sew, it will show. We will squeeze the needle out of you for lying."

Tobias was supposed to give me instructions and to make sure the work was done properly. He watched me remove the old braid, and watched as I replaced every stitch by hand. I did the work very carefully, just as I had learned as a young apprentice.

When I finished the sewing, I was given an iron and I pressed the uniform. It was lucky for me that I gave the jacket a "once over" before the job was finished, because I found two lice on the collar of the jacket. They were quite alive and ready to cause trouble. When the Oberfeldfabel inspected the work he asked Tobias if I had done it by machine. Tobias told him that it was by hand. He seemed incredulous. He was so impressed that he ordered Tobias to arrange to have me assigned as his tailor. He then wrote out an order stating that my work was to be done solely for him and for a few other officers that he would designate from time to time. He added that I was not to be assigned for normal work details, but should report directly to his headquarters.

Up until that point I had been working with the other inmates of Kaufering at Moll, where the Nazis were building an underground aircraft factory. It was some nine levels deep and heavily guarded. There were bomb shelters on every level. My job was to work on scaffolding with an air hammer. It was a dangerous job. Many of the other inmates had lost their balance and fallen to their deaths. After each shift, we would have to carry the dead back to the camp for "inventory." Because of the high mortality rate, some of the inmates would hide in the morning to avoid inclusion in these crews. We were always hoping for less dangerous assignments, so I considered myself lucky to have the opportunity to return to tailoring.

A few days after we arrived, a group of prominent Czech leaders from Prague were placed with us. Many had been government employees, engineers, professors, writers, and doctors. While at Kaufering they had worked with the rest of us at Moll.

The Czechs were not used to a life of deprivation and physical stress, and they couldn't take the hard labor, the lice, the horrible diet, and the hunger. As a result they became very depressed, and almost 80 percent of these Christian Czechs killed themselves by jumping in front of the small train which was used to carry materials to the underground factory. The remaining twenty percent died from disease. As far as I know, none survived to liberation.

Life was much easier for me once I began working for the Oberfeldfabel, and I must admit that I was treated better than almost all the other inmates at Kaufering. That is not to say that my life was easy, quite the contrary; work in the tailor shop exposed me to a new danger.

# chapter 19

F

rom the beginning, the tailor shop was set up to serve only the elite officers of the military assigned to the camp. Soon I was put in charge of a laundry
as well, operated by a Jewish woman from Hungary who was assisted by several
young women. Both the laundry and the tailor shop were inspected frequently
by an SS Sturmbannführer named Schumacher. He was dangerous. He had been
an organizer for the Nazi party since its inception, and he hated Jews.

Schumacher would always come into the tailor shop hoping to find unauthorized work. The punishment for getting caught could be hanging. He would
literally turn the place upside down in his searches and would leave only when
he could find nothing wrong. One of the warrant officers had warned me about
Schumacher. Even the Germans were afraid of him, not only because of his rank
but because of his strong Nazi connections.

I was very busy in the shop making clothes, for the officers, and their families. Because my skills were in demand, I could ask for certain items to which
no other inmate had access. Surprisingly, there was some medical care available
to inmates at Kaufering. A small "hospital" had been set up and staffed by doctors, although they had few supplies or medical instruments. I became acquainted
with a sergeant who was able to get medicines. He brought me dysentery medi-
cation when I was sick and also helped me get other pills and aspirin, which I
smuggled back to the barracks and gave to the other inmates. Schumacher had

apparently overlooked the fact that I was allowed to go between the tailor shop and the barracks without being searched.

There was a barrel in my shop that contained powdered soap for the SS soldiers to use for their laundry. Schumacher warned us not to permit anyone to take the soap without authorization. Still, many soldiers would stop into the shop and take a scoop or two before leaving. Despite our pleadings, it was impossible for us to refuse them. At Kaufering even the rank and file SS weren't given enough food, and they traded soap for produce from the local farmers. One day Schumacher inspected the shop and noticed that the soap barrel was only half full. He demanded to know what had happened to the rest of the soap, and I lied, telling him that the kitchen women took it for washing laundry. "You are lucky this time," he said and walked away.

One day while I was working, Tobias told me about his boss, the Oberfeld-fabel. He said the man had many friends in high places and used his connections to retain his Wehrmacht status and wasn't forced to join the SS as were the other camp administrators. Before being assigned to Kaufering he had been wounded at the Russian front.

I noticed after a while, that many soldiers didn't eat their bread crusts, so one day I asked Dietermann if someone could gather them up so that I could take them to the other inmates. Although I usually had enough to eat because of my work for the Oberfeldfabel, these crusts were desperately needed by other inmates to keep them alive. It was very important to get as much food as possible, no matter how little its nutritional value might be. Dietermann agreed to help me on the condition that these crust collections would only occur when Schumacher wasn't around.

One day in December of 1944, we were all assembled so that the owner of the aircraft assembly plant could select one hundred strong men for a special project. Even though the Oberfeldfabel told me not to worry about the "selec-tion" for the new work assignment, the guards lined us up, myself as well as my friend Brzezinski, who was my helper in the tailor shop. Luckily, we weren't among those chosen. Camp 7 was being closed and Brzezinski and I were to be transferred to Camp 3 before the group left. The others from our barrack in Camp 7 who had been "selected" were sent to help dig a huge tunnel near Berlin. After the war I learned that only five of the original hundred men sent to work there had survived the project.

When we arrived at the new camp the Oberfeldfabel told our new Blockälteste that I was his personal tailor and that Brzezinski was my assistant and that we were to be treated well. We remained in Camp 3 for only a few days. We were moved to Camp 4, then back to Camp 3, and Camp 1. All these transfers were taking place because the Oberfeldfabel was getting different assignments and he was doing all he could to keep me nearby. Finally, though, he was reassigned away from all the camps. He visited me at my latest tailor shop in Camp 1 and told me that a second lieutenant, a doctor, would be my new unofficial sponsor. He said that he had told the doctor of my skills and that it would be wise for him to take good care of me. After that, I never saw him again.

Some of the old faces stayed on, however, including Schumacher who was now in charge of Camps 3 and 4. Schumacher still wielded power in the administration of the camps and the doctor submitted many of his decisions to Schumacher for his advice and approval. In camp, I heard new stories from other inmates about Schumacher's cruelty. These stories were confirmed by my own observations. Once I witnessed the execution of a forty-year-old man and his twenty-year-old son. They had been accused of sabotage and we were told that they had been tried by the Nazis and found guilty. They weren't told what the "sabotage" was, but we found out later that all they had done was try to make shoes out of some blankets. They were hanged on the gallows in full view of the crowd. Schumacher urged us to "picture" this scene in our minds and "never forget it." We had to watch the two men climb up on two barrels with ropes around their necks. The ropes were tied snugly, and at Schumacher's order the barrels were kicked out from under them. "Never forget it," he said. I never have.

The greatest threat to my safety came from Schumacher and his constant suspicions of me. He still tried to catch me tailoring for unauthorized patrons. He would strike like a lightning bolt, looking everywhere for evidence of illegal work or for contraband. I never knew whether he had any evidence that I was working unlawfully or if he just wanted to keep us off guard. The truth was that I had been doing lots of extra work, especially for the Ukrainian guards who paid me with extra bread. They would throw their clothes over the barbed-wire fence and, when the tailoring was finished, I would throw them back.

One day Schumacher came into the shop in a particularly angry mood. He started searching the place, and I was sure he had heard that I was working on some jobs for the Ukrainians. By the time he left he had turned the place upside down and the shop was a mess, but I was lucky. He hadn't bothered to bend down to look at the bottom of the storage cabinets where I had hidden the Ukrainians' uniforms. My unauthorized work was a dangerous risk to take for a little bread and some medicines, but I had learned that in order to survive in the camps one had to take such chances to stay alive.

Another time, Schumacher ordered the inmates of my barrack to line up to inspect our teeth for gold and diamonds. A German kapo walked up and down the lines accompanied by an SS guard. When they reached me the kapo ordered me to open my mouth wide. He noticed that I had a gold crown on one of my front teeth, and before I knew what he was doing he had taken a wrench and knocked out all of my front teeth with one swift blow. As I stood there, in shock and in incredible pain, he calmly ordered me to spit out the tooth fragments into a small container. Later they would separate the gold from the teeth.

◆ ◆ ◆

For the most part, the only news we heard about the war was optimistic Nazi propaganda. One day, for example, Tobias came into the tailor shop and told me he had a "happy announcement" to make. He said that the Americans were suffering heavy losses and that he was sure "We are going to win! And Schneider-meister," he added, "I have even more wonderful news." I was afraid to ask what that might be. "We have a secret weapon and we will win the war by the first of the year." I broke into a cold sweat when I heard this news.

A few days later, on a Sunday, all the inmates were ordered out of the bar-racks into formation. Over the loudspeaker an announcement was made about how the Germans would totally demolish the Allies and would soon win the war with their "wonder weapon." All the Nazis had to do was set it up and use it. No details about this weapon were given, but such information would have been meaningless to us anyway. More important was our fear that the Germans might be justified in their new-found confidence. They were predicting the de-struction of American cities and a total victory for Hitler. Some of us had dared to believe the Germans were indeed losing the war. Now we realized anew how precarious our existence was. Many of us felt that we were now in more danger than we had ever been since we left Auschwitz.

Dietermann did not realize the effect his "good news" would have on us. He was as close to a friend as we had, and merely wanted to share something positive with us. Shortly after Dietermann told us about his "good news," the wife of a warrant officer called me in and said, "Carl, I have good news for you." I wasn't sure I wanted to hear any more "good news," but I was curious, so I asked her, "What is it?"

She told me that because the Nazis were winning the war she and her husband had started planning what they would do when the war was over and life returned to normal. "You will be with us to the end of your life," she said, "and you will be our family tailor. You will do all the work for us. In other words, you will not be killed and there will be no concentration camp for you after the war be-cause each of us will be allowed to take some of the younger inmates with us. But," she continued, "the Nazis have said that all who are kept alive as servants will have to be castrated."

My insides went into convulsions. I almost stopped breathing for a while, and

I said to myself, "God, is that what you are going to do to your children," or what we call "Bnai-Israel," the children of Israel. I felt weak and sick. After having suffered through all these years I was to survive as a castrated slave!

She told me that they would also be taking a Hungarian Jewish woman as a maid. The young lady was about twenty-one, very intelligent and had been in charge of the laundry for the SS troops. She spoke four or five languages. The warrant officer's wife said that the maid would also be sterilized so that there would be no possibility of producing children.

I told her that I appreciated her kindness in thinking so highly of me, but that I really wasn't interested in the life she proposed. She told me how good their life would be, and she confirmed a story I had heard from Dietermann that her husband was a much-decorated hero and would be entitled to the good life after the war. He would receive a large tract of land and a certain number of slaves, according to his rank and his contributions to the Nazi cause.

As far as I knew, most of the other inmates in the camp weren't aware of these possibilities or of the deals I had been offered. Some, I am sure, would have taken their risks, as I did, and said no to such favors. Others who were young and only feared death might have agreed to these conditions. I am not aware of any other inmates who were told about their prospects after the war, had the Germans won. Of course, many of our group were over thirty and wouldn't have been offered the chance to live as a castrated slave.

◆ ◆ ◆

Inmates who worked closely with the Germans were often reminded that we could not use the indoor toilets. It was strictly forbidden and the penalty, of course, could be death. While working in the tailor shop we had no place to relieve ourselves without risking punishment. Dietermann advised us to use our minor privileges of freedom of movement within the camp to solve our problem.

At this time, the tailor shop was located in a building that also housed the laundry and storage facilities of the SS troops, across the street from their living quarters. Every day SS guards would escort me from the prison camp to the tailor shop and back again. Near the building where the tailor shop was located, there were some trees and small bushes. Some of the trees could have been used at Christmas. Freedom was such a short distance away; beyond the trees was a fence marking the boundary of the SS camp. But Tobias had warned me, "Don't run away." If I was caught, he assured me, there would be no saving me from hanging. He told me to just go out and take care of my needs, cover my presence there, and come back to the tailor shop.

Looking into the woods, I could see the "corners of freedom," and I could not help thinking about escape. In fact, it was impossible and capture almost certain. A young Russian prisoner of war, no more than twenty-five years old, had run away only a couple of days after the father and son had been hanged for sabotage. The Russian was caught when he stopped at a farmhouse to beg for food. The people in the house tied him up and turned him over to the gendarmes. The Nazis hanged him, even though he wasn't a Jew. Still, dreaming of escape was a way of mentally fighting back and maintaining some shred of self-confidence. Just getting close to a means of freedom gave me some hope of getting out of camp.

◆ ◆ ◆

All the time we were at Kaufering, the Americans had been dropping leaflets which fell on the fields around the camp. Sometimes inmates would pick them up as they came back from Moll. Of course, reading such propaganda was against the rules of the camp, and anyone caught doing so would be shot or hanged. But we were so desperate for any news, any glimmer of hope, that many took the risk, hiding the forbidden papers as best they could.

One of the best hiding places was in the soles of what passed for shoes. Inmates were so wretched that the guards simply did not check the foot coverings, so that we could protect such contraband from the frequent searches. In the barrack the leaflets were inspiring. By the light of a single dim bulb, we read the Allied leaflets proclaiming their imminent victory, appealing to the Germans to lay down their arms, and threatening much suffering if the war continued.

The Allied propaganda raised many questions, and many of us asked ourselves, "How can God help us to survive the end of the war?" It was apparent to most of us that we were caught in a web from which we could never escape by ourselves. We speculated about the course of the war and about our chances for survival, and often these thoughts distracted us from the daily humiliations and brutality of the camp.

Once, when I was relieving myself in the bushes by the tailor shop I saw a rat and then a mouse pass. Then another small rodent—I didn't know what it was—passed and stopped. It looked at me intently, then ran off. At that time I wished I could become a rat or a mouse so that I could just crawl out of that camp like these other rodents. My favorite fantasy was to become a bird, spread my wings, and fly off to the Tyrol mountains that I could see from the tailor shop. When the sun shone on the mountains, it stirred me, and my heart beat faster while I asked myself, "Why? Why couldn't I be a bird or an animal that could leave the camp at will?"

# chapter 20

On Christmas Eve of 1944, all the healthy inmates were herded into a large social hall. The hall was truly beautiful. It had been elaborately decorated for the Christmas celebration. After a large number of Polish males were in place, an equal number of Hungarian women were brought in. Most of the men had not been close to a woman for a long time because it was against the rules of the camp.

A Christmas tree had been erected and decorated with the "iron crosses" that symbolized the Nazi regime. Much effort and time had obviously been spent on decorating the place and it was apparent that those responsible had strong Christian roots. Perhaps the SS woman in charge helped coordinate the decorating. One thing that attracted our attention besides the Christmas tree was a cross that hung in a warm light, exuding a wonderful reflection.

The SS woman in charge said to us, "We have called you in to celebrate Christmas Eve," implying that we should enjoy ourselves and the celebration of the birth of Christ. She said, "We want you to understand that tonight is one which touches every human being, so we want you to enjoy it with us." In her efforts to make us feel like celebrating, the SS woman insisted that we sing Christmas carols. The songs were not familiar to us, but she said, "I want you to sing *Oh Holy Night* and *Tannenbaum*." The inmates were saddened rather than cheered by the celebration and could not bring themselves to sing a single note. The SS woman also told us we could kneel at the Christmas tree. Most of us just stood in our places, confused and bewildered at the strangeness of the occasion. Finally, the woman ordered us to kneel.

The hall was very warm in contrast to the conditions we were used to. Soon, the unaccustomed warmth of our bodies roused the lice that were hidden, dormant, in our clothes and on our bodies. There must have been dozens of them under my shirt. Actually we would have been much more comfortable if we had stayed in the cold. It tended to keep the lice inactive. The parasites in a frenzy made us very uncomfortable.

After the Christmas carols, the woman in charge passed out candies. It was the first time in more than five years that many of us had eaten any candy. We moaned to ourselves, "How long can this torture go on?" As the evening wore on, we were told over and over again how well we were being treated. "Blessed with kindness," the SS woman said. Never in my wildest nightmares did I ever dream of such "blessings" that we were told we were receiving. At last they released us, but not before we had each received another handful of candy and some black cookies. We went back to the barrack to ponder the evening's events and fight off the ravenous lice.

After Christmas, life went on very much as usual in Camp 3. The weather was very cold and living in the filthy barrack claimed forty to fifty lives every day. We stacked the bodies much in the same way as we had while traveling in the cattle trains. At any one time there may have been as many as thirty-five or forty corpses piled up outside our barrack walls. Another problem was that some of the inmates, desperate for more food, kept their neighbors' bodies in their bunks so they could receive the dead inmates' rations. After a while, the corpses began to really stink up the barrack.

The corpses that were outside were frozen solid. It may have been as cold as ten below zero. At least there was one advantage to the frigid weather—it destroyed some of the lice. It was one of the small things that seemed so vitally important at the time.

◆ ◆ ◆

On January 1, 1945, we were given the day off. The only activity was an inventory of the living and the dead. After that we were assembled by a SS *Gruppenführer*, the equivalent of a sergeant. He seemed particularly compassionate towards us, an unusual attitude for an SS man in the camps. While he was in charge, there were fewer beatings and much less cruelty towards us.

At noon the SS Gruppenführer addressed us. "Today is the first of January 1945, the first day of the year and I am wishing you luck. Luck that the Jews will be liberated and that you can live as the righteous human beings that you are.

I wish you a happy year and a hope for your freedom. The sun shall shine on you as on other races."

This was a bizarre speech for an SS man to make. We did not know what to do or how to react. They were powerful, moving words, but desperate as we were for any news that could give us hope, we had too often known the bitterness of disappointment, and we could not let ourselves become too optimistic. Nevertheless, this particular man had done what he could to make life better for us, so I became hopeful that we might survive, after all. Not long afterwards, I heard an astonishing story that partly explained this man's attitude towards his prisoners.

◆ ◆ ◆

Those inmates chosen to serve the guards, soldiers, and administrators of the camp were housed in a barrack apart from the other prisoners. Most were called "transport kommandos," and were generally assigned to menial labor. There were about twenty-five of these transport kommandos in the barrack, plus a few others who, like me, were particularly skilled. There were barbers, office workers, an accountant, a jeweler, a goldsmith, and some artists. We had hot water for shaving, and we were allowed to bathe from a bucket. We also had a little extra food because the transport kommandos were able to steal extra bread and potatoes. We even had a small stove that we were allowed to use for cooking. Ours was the only barrack where such privileges were permitted. Even our bedding was changed from time to time to help us stay free of lice, although we were never entirely free of the vermin. There was always work, but there was also time for talk, and we told many stories. Some were true no doubt, others may have been only partly so.

Among the transport kommandos were a father and his two sons who came from Vilna, the capital of Lithuania. It was the father who told me the story about the SS Gruppenführer. "You know," he once whispered to me," that SS man is responsible for my two sons and I being together." That was odd; families were usually separated in the camps.

He went on to tell me that the SS man was the illegitimate son of Christian parents in Vilna. His mother did not want him, and he was given to a Jewish man who raised him as one of his own. This man already had five children, two boys and three girls, and the adopted child was given the same rearing as his own children, although he was not circumcised. By the time the boy was seventeen, he was working as a driver in his adoptive father's beer distributorship. He was a fully accepted member of the family, but was not forced to become a practicing Jew. When the war broke out, he still lived with the family.

Lithuania was occupied first by the Russians and then by the Germans.

After the German invasion, it was no longer safe for the boy to live with this Jewish family, so the young man went away. Apparently he joined the German police force, and later entered the army. He must have claimed that at least one of his parents was a true German, because eventually he joined the SS. Ironically, he was present when the family that raised him was taken into captivity. Without the young man's help, the transporter said, he and his sons would never have survived.

The Jew who told me this story was the SS Gruppenführer's adoptive father. He told me that as the family was moved from one camp to the next, the young man somehow was able to get himself assigned to the same camp, and in each place, he secretly helped make life easier for them as well as for other Jews. This transport kommando owed his life and the lives of his sons to the SS Gruppenführer's help in keeping them together and getting them assigned as transport kommandos with the better treatment that that job entailed. As I listened to the story, many things that had puzzled me began to make sense. I thought about how the SS Gruppenführer would come into the tailor shop and, when he had work for me, would pay me with bread, salami, and margarine, and would ask me to take some to the other inmates. I know, too, that he had done other favors for Jews in the camp. He was a relatively kind man who had taken risks to be sure that his adoptive father and brothers were not selected for the wrong group when the camps were liquidated. If the transport kommando's story was true, then in all the madness of the Nazis' quest to develop a racially pure world they had overlooked a minor SS member who owed his life to a family of Jews. In spite of all their power, there were glaring chinks in the Nazis' armor which permitted some to survive in the face of overwhelming odds.

I was separated from the father and son in a later reorganization of the camps, and I lost contact with them for a while. I do know, however, that they survived, at least until the American army arrived to liberate us. The liberation made the SS Gruppenführer's best wishes a reality for some of us, but many died between January and May 2 of 1945. It still amazes me that within the structure of the Nazi machine that tried to destroy a race, there was a man who had been raised by a Jewish family and was willing to help Jews while serving the Germans.

◆ ◆ ◆

The routine of bartering for bread, medicine, and other goods in exchange for my tailoring kept me very busy going from barrack to barrack and back to the tailor shop. One day I met a man who looked completely out of place. He was well into his sixties, perhaps sixty-five or older, and he was dressed in a fine suit and tie and wore well-made Polish dress shoes. I was curious about this newcomer and wanted to find out who he was and why he was here. I greeted him in German and, hoping to start a conversation, commented that his well-dressed appearance in a death camp barrack was unusual.

He told me that his name was Dr. Berliner and that he had been a professor of medicine at the Berlin University's medical school. He had lived for some time under house arrest in Berlin, and had only recently been sent to a concentration camp. He asked me about myself and listened while I told him about my Polish roots, my life in the various camps, especially Auschwitz, and how I had come to be a tailor for the SS in this camp.

Dr. Berliner in turn told me about his life under house arrest. Though he had been allowed to live in an apartment near the university, his life had been totally controlled by the Nazis. His family had been taken away at the beginning of the war and he had not seen them again. His food was brought to him, and he could travel only between his home and the university. He could not receive mail or use the telephone. In December of 1944, when the Russians had started their offensive towards Berlin, the Nazis had sent him to Kaufering without even the small privileges he had been allowed in his former life. His clean, neat appearance, as if he had just come from a wedding, was the only reminder of his former existence. He did, however, have a private room in the barrack, and he had met Dr. Bromberg, the Polish doctor from Bialystok. As we talked I began to realize that this gentle, well-educated man was ill-prepared for camp life.

Dr. Berliner asked me about Dachau, and I told him it meant the end of each of our lives. Despair was hard to fight. If we had any hope of liberation, we could survive more easily. But for most of us, I told him, the future looked very bleak and hopeless. To survive would be a miracle of indescribable magnitude. We shook hands, and I returned to my work.

The next time I heard about Dr. Berliner, he was helping inmates who were sick or injured. An SS Lieutenant who had been his student in 1940, had arranged for Dr. Berliner along with Dr. Bromberg to perform surgery on inmates. The medical facilities were crude. The operating room contained a large galvanized iron tub, which was filled with water and then heated in order to sterilize instruments and dressings. It was amazing that an SS officer would allow operations or any medical care for inmates. Dr. Berliner was even permitted to visit the barracks and check on sick inmates and to keep medical records.

Whenever Dr. Berliner took medical histories in the barrack he would ask each male patient, "When was the last time you had an erection?" Answers varied from "not for a long time," to "not since becoming an inmate." The doctor faithfully recorded each answer.

Most of the inmates in my barrack were healthy in contrast to others. Dr. Berliner examined everyone there and asked each of us questions about our sexual interest. When it was my turn I told him that I frequently had an erection, sometimes as often as a few mornings in a row or sometimes when I was just resting. I asked Dr. Berliner why he was so interested in our sexual experience. He did not answer directly, but told me that from his extensive medical knowledge, he felt that men who no longer had frequent erections had also lost their will to live. The "vitamins" that help men to live had been lost, and when illness struck, death would be close behind.

A short time later, Camp 3 was closed and those of us left alive were transferred back to Camp 1. Dr. Berliner was moved from Camp 4 to Camp 3. Then he also went to Camp 1. There he cared for some patients who could not walk. Later, the Germans executed those who could not move to another camp under their own power, and Dr. Berliner may have been executed with them. When the war was over, I could find no trace of him.

◆ ◆ ◆

On Passover in 1945, a dozen of us got together for prayers. We did not know it at the time, but it was to be our last religious celebration as slaves of the Nazis. Among our group was a very Orthodox rabbi from the Seven Mountain area of Numkasz. He was a wonderful human being, and we took great care to make sure that he did not suffer too much or starve. As Passover approached, he helped organize the observance.

On Passover eve, we celebrated with the traditional seder dinner, which commemorates the time of Jewish captivity in Egypt. Inmates who worked outside the camp were somehow able to obtain dark, heavy flour, probably by begging from the local farmers. They carried this into the camp in their dirty clothes, in their pockets, and under their waist bands, and slowly we stored up a supply. By the time the seder drew near, we had enough flour to bake a few matzos, the unleavened bread that Jews eat during Passover. We baked the matzos in the stove which was used to heat the irons in my tailor shop. If the unleavened bread or any of the other preparations had been noticed, there was no doubt that we would have been killed.

To avoid discovery, we could not use the lights. There was a small window in the barrack's door and we could not risk being observed. Even so, we did not celebrate in total darkness. Using the same ingenuity we employed to gather the flour, we were also able to get a few candles from the German people. We covered the window with a rag, posted a sentry outside, and proceeded with our celebration of Passover. Fortunately, the Ukrainian guards would not enter the barracks unless there was a disturbance. If all remained quiet, they would stay in the towers near the perimeter of the camp.

The rabbi began the Passover ritual with the words that recounted the Jewish slavery in Egypt. "And this is the moment of our last days of existence," the rabbi said. He recited the entire ceremony from memory and the celebration went on for a couple of hours, right through to midnight. He broke the matzo and gave each of us a piece, and then we prayed. We left as much matzo as we could, hoping that the rabbi would take it. He had been fasting for eight days. Before that we had given him potatoes to sustain him, and he was grateful for that, but he was not a particularly strong man to begin with. The rest of us had been eating whatever we could obtain. The rabbi put his faith before personal needs. I had great respect for him because he was willing to sacrifice his health and his life for his religion. He lived up to the letter and the spirit of the Talmud.

◆ ◆ ◆

As the days passed, we began to hear more news of the Allied advance, and it became frighteningly clear that we might be killed before the Germans surrendered. My tailoring was curtailed, and I was assigned to a heavy construction project at an underground airplane factory.

After working there for a short time, I met another benevolent SS man who helped me get a job feeding and herding cows. The cattle had been brought to the area by Hungarian refugees hoping to save themselves and their kine from the advancing Russian army. The Germans had made good use of the cows, scattering them over the entire area to camouflage the airplane factory. Seeing cattle grazing peacefully on the green hillsides, the Allied pilots would not guess that there was a war plane factory underground.

# chapter 21

By late April of 1945, the American army was making significant progress. We were assembled and ordered to march out of the camp. Fathers called out in vain, trying, in the confusion, to make contact with their sons. On the road from Kaufering to Dachau there was much screaming and crying. Heavy army trucks were speeding down the roads and, in their reckless haste, ran over many of the marchers. In the first hour of the march, I saw at least four bodies that were smashed to bits, strewn all over the highway by the retreating trucks. After about three hours of marching, we were allowed to stop and rest. It was already quite late at night, and we sought shelter in the trees alongside the highway. As we rested, we discussed all the rumors we had heard. A few of us thought we would all be shot before the end of the march, but no one had any reliable information.

We continued marching for two more days until we reached Dachau. We spent only one day and one night there, sleeping in a field at the camp. Then we were each given a piece of bread and marched out of the camp in the direction of Innsbruck.

In our group, there were many Poles, as well as large numbers of Russians and Lithuanians. We tried to mingle with the nationalities in different groups so that the Germans would not be able to easily wipe out any particular nationality. Of course, we didn't know if they intended to do so, but we didn't want to take the chance. I was in a group consisting mostly of non-Jewish Poles and found Dr. Bromberg among us. He was actually very lucky to have been there because his barrack had been doused with gasoline or kerosene and ignited just hours before the American advance. Many of the inmates were burned alive and others were shot as they tried to escape.

By April 30th we had been marching for several days. Dr. Bromberg was so weak he could hardly walk, and the SS men were shooting those who could not keep up with the columns, and throwing their bodies into the ditches by the side of the road. Dr. Bromberg, with tears in his eyes, begged me, "Please, don't let them kill me, drag me by the armpits." Srulek Brezinski and I did this, and, after a mile or so, we rested. The rest was truly a lifesaver, because the doctor was able to regain enough strength to walk by himself.

Dr. Bromberg had been with us at Blizyn. At that camp he was not permitted to work as a doctor, but was assigned to breaking up stones. His wife, a trained nurse, worked in the hospital. From Blizyn they were taken to Auschwitz where the men and women were kept in separate barracks, each with its own field. These fields were separated by an electrified fence. Dr. Bromberg and his wife were allowed to speak to each other once a day through the fence. One day she didn't appear. He learned that she was sick with appendicitis and desperately in need of surgery. With the help of other inmates, he disguised himself as a plumber and was smuggled into the women's barracks where he operated on his wife and saved her life. Bromberg's wife was a Christian and could have left him when he was sent to the camps, but she didn't. She was dedicated to her husband, and when he was taken by the Germans, she went with him to die, if necessary, by his side. They were separated when he was sent to Kaufering.

We marched all day, and that night we slept by the side of the road. The next morning, the SS received instructions to free us, but within two hours the headquarters in Berlin rescinded the order. We were recaptured and forced to continue marching all that day. As we walked we could hear the Germans and the Americans fighting. The Germans were in front of us, the Americans at our rear. We acted as a buffer zone. At one point, we had to cross a rather long bridge. As soon as we did, it was blown up, presumably by the Nazis trying to slow the American advance.

I don't remember how long we had been marching when we reached the mountains, perhaps two days, maybe three. We began to climb, and the Germans took up positions that would give them an advantage over the advancing army. But the German weapons posed no defense against the American tanks, and the Germans continued to retreat. From time to time they stopped to fight, using whatever cover was available.

Even in retreat, our guards continued their brutality. I remember a young inmate who asked one of the guards if he could stop for a moment and go into the fields to relieve his stomach cramps. The guard gave his permission, and then shot him as soon as he squatted in the field. Some of the guards were German, but most were Ukrainian, and they were the most brutal. The guard who shot that young man was Ukrainian.

Although the Germans were using trucks, many of the personal effects of the SS were being transported in two and three wheeled trailers drawn by humans. The trailers were piled high with baggage and knapsacks. It took four or five strong men to pull each trailer, and even then the strain was enormous. Those who stumbled and fell were beaten and others were forced to replace them.

Even though we tried to keep our groups mixed while marching, at night we regrouped by national origin. We were each given a piece of bread, margarine, and sometimes a little marmalade. By that time there were fewer and fewer German guards, and those who were left were overworked and tired. At night, they went to sleep and left the prisoners alone. One evening after receiving our rations, a group of Russian inmates attacked us, hoping to get our food. We in turn armed ourselves with clubs of heavy wooden sticks gathered nearby. About twenty-five of us attacked the Russians, and beat them soundly. Then we returned to our resting places as if nothing had happened.

On the morning of May 1, we were marching toward the city of Bat Tüllz. While we stopped and rested, the Germans made us a strange offer. We would be given weapons, hand grenades, and food, if we would put on German uniforms and fight the Americans. In the hour of their defeat, the Germans had asked us—their victims—to fight against our liberators. None of the Jews agreed to this request, although a few of the non-Jewish prisoners did. I don't know what happened to them because we left them behind and continued on our march. Along the way we passed several small German tanks with guns aimed back towards the advancing American army. As we passed the German tanks, we prayed for their destruction.

Our stop that night was on much higher ground, well into the mountains. It was already dusk when we stopped. Just after sunset it began to snow, lightly at first, and then heavily. The Germans ordered us to lie down. By morning the snow was almost a foot high. We were very hungry and cold. We ate the snow to curb our appetites. I had an overcoat which gave me some protection, but many had almost nothing to keep out the cold. Somehow my coat had survived all the shifting from camp to camp.

When I awoke, I realized that Dr. Bromberg was nearby, and I also recognized Israel Brzezinki. As we lay near each other in the snow, we talked about all the time we had spent together since 1943 in Blizyn. Then we began to speculate about what the Germans had in store for us. We both agreed it was getting close to the end of the line for both of us. Suddenly, we heard a very clear voice ask in German for the "commander-in-charge." I raised my head to see what was going on. One of the guards said that the commander was "in the house over there," and pointed to a typical Tyrol mountain farmhouse.

The intruder bellowed, "I want you to go and wake your commander and report to me immediately." The guard complied and returned a few minutes later, saying that the commander, an Obersturmführer in the SS, did not want to arise at the time, and when he did so, it would take some time to get ready and dressed. The intruder spoke very loudly again, telling the guard that he was a general officer and was in charge of the entire war effort in the region. The man claiming to be the territorial commander looked impressive. He had at least three lower-ranking assistants. We could plainly recognize the rank from his epaulets as he stood waiting in the snow, and we wondered what his presence there could mean.

When our commander finally appeared, he reported with a snappy *"Heil Hitler,"* which was not acknowledged. Even from where we lay in the snow, we could sense the tension between them. The general wanted to know who we were and why we were there. The commander told him that we were part of a group of about forty thousand inmates from camps in the Dachau area, and that he needed further orders as to our destination before he could proceed with the march.

We heard the general say, "I am ordering you to leave the inmates here. Do not go any further. The enemy is on our land, and they are occupying Germany. This is not our territory. The enemy will have the right to do what they want. You will be personally responsible for marching these people from Dachau and for murdering some and leaving them to die along the ditches and roads." The "transport commander" replied that he could not take orders from an army officer, only from SS headquarters. Their voices were very loud as they argued. Finally, the "transport commander" put his hand on the pistol in his holster. Instantly, the general's aides drew their weapons and pointed them at the Obersturmführer before he had a chance to shoot the general. The general quietly insisted that his opponent turn over his weapon. The commander refused, and was cautioned about the consequences. After some more arguing, however, the Obersturmführer complied and the general's men arrested him and took him away.

During the confrontation, Dr. Bromberg stood up and brushed off the snow. He was very weak, but he managed to make his way down the slope to where the general stood. When he reached him, he said, "I am Dr. Bromberg. I need help to save my life. I am cold and sick, and very hungry. I beg you to help me and all the others. I don't think we can last any longer without some aid. I beg you, as commanding officer and a fellow human being, to help us." The general responded to Dr. Bromberg's request, called for an army ambulance, and the doctor was taken away. Earlier on the march, he had confided to me that if he were released he intended to return to Poland to try to find his wife. He was sure she was still alive. He hugged me and said, "Carl, I will see you when I come back with my wife."

It seemed only a few minutes later that we were ordered to start marching again. After about an hour, we arrived at a small German village with exceptionally beautiful houses. The town must have had many rich inhabitants. The Germans opened the doors of a large barn and ordered some three hundred of us to go inside. The barn had some light inside, but, except for a lot of scattered straw and hay, there was little in the way of comfort. There was no food or water, and the Germans specifically ordered us not to relieve ourselves inside the barn. Then they locked us in and stationed guards outside the door.

Inside we could hear the heavy artillery echoing between the mountains and the foothills. The shooting was almost continuous throughout the night. We knew that the Americans were advancing rapidly and we wondered whether this might be the last day of our captivity.

The barn had a door that connected with the landowner's living quarters. One of his employees was a French laborer who smuggled water in to us, along with bread and some other food. The Frenchman told us he thought liberation was very near.

As morning came, the shooting stopped. We were so used to the sounds of war that the quiet was disconcerting. The barn's doors were still locked from the outside. We were not sure if the SS guards were still there, but we knew that if they were, they would surely shoot us if we tried to escape. As it grew lighter, a few of the inmates climbed up to the loft to get a better view of our situation. They told us that the guards had deserted their posts. We wondered if it was a trap. So we waited. Suddenly, at about 9 o'clock, we heard strange noises. We could hear heavy equipment, tanks perhaps, coming towards us. The sound was very exciting, and we urged the lookouts to climb as high into the loft as they could and report what they could see. They said that they could see tanks, and that these were coming nearer, and then finally, they shouted that the tanks had white stars painted on them! The Americans were approaching the village.

Our lookouts climbed down, and we decided to break open the door. Although there were 300 men in the barn, breaking it down was no easy task. It was well built, and we were very weak men. But no one wanted to wait to be discovered. We gathered all our strength and together we forced the door open by rocking against it.

We ran out into the yard and cried, "We are free! We are free!" No one was there to hear us, but it was the most wonderful sound we had ever heard.

The tanks were traveling on a highway about five hundred meters from the barn. We ran as fast as we could until some of the soldiers noticed us and stopped. They warned us not to get too close to the tanks. I remember one American soldier who stuck his head out from the tank's turret and said in German, "You are free now. We are American soldiers and must move on, so please do not block our way." Others threw us candy, apples, and oranges, and there was such a tangle of men trying to catch something, that some of the newly freed men were injured.

The Americans told us that the ground troops were about seven kilometers behind. "They will help you," they said. "We must keep going after the Germans." With that, they rumbled off in hot pursuit.

## chapter 22

**N**o words can describe my feelings at the moment of liberation. Once I realized I was free and alive, I began to think of all my fellow inmates who had fallen and died during the march. And I thought of all those who were killed in the gas chambers and those who had died of disease, starvation, and torture in the camps.

In our race to the highway to meet the advancing Americans, some of the inmates had fallen in the field. The snow had melted and the ground was wet and muddy, and they had no strength to get up. We went back to give them the good news of our liberation. I remember one who opened his eyes and said, "Yes, I am free," and then closed them forever. There were many others who died in that field and in other areas nearby, exhausted by the years of effort to survive.

Even in our weakened state, however, the liberation was very exciting. As we explored our surroundings, we came upon weapons abandoned by the Germans. With a rifle in my hands, I decided to retaliate against the Nazis. I was ready to kill any one of them I could find. I promised myself that I would go from door to door and kill. It would not really matter if they were innocent civilians. They were guilty, and I would be their executioner. There must be revenge and payment for all the suffering we had endured.

After a short search, I found ammunition for the rifle. It had fallen a short distance from where I found the gun. I loaded it quickly. It was an easy task for an ex-machine gunner in the Polish army. The hard part lay ahead. With the gun slung over my shoulder, I began to walk back towards Bat Tüllz. But I was so weak that carrying the rifle taxed my strength. I fell to the ground and decided that I really did not want the weapon, after all, so I left it in a ditch and headed for a nearby farmhouse, weak but exhilarated by my new freedom. I was free. I had no plans for the future, no idea of what would become of me, but I was free.

There was only one person in the farmhouse, a disabled army veteran, sitting in a makeshift wheelchair. He was a pathetic sight, moving about on a board with wheels. "Tell me about yourself," I asked. He told me he was a former German officer who had fought against the Americans. He had been badly wounded, and the doctors had amputated both his legs to save his life. He spent six months as a prisoner, and was returned to Germany in a prisoner exchange. I demanded to know if he had killed any Jews during the occupation of France.

"Kill me if you want to," he said. "My life is not worth anything." He condemned the Nazis and the terror they had brought to millions, and finally he said that he had nothing to do with killing Jews.

"Yes, I could kill you," I told him, "and keep a promise I made to myself that I would kill every German I found after the war was over and I was liberated. You are so pitiful, I can not take your life." He cried and I cried. I was hungry, but I left without taking any of his food. I just locked the door and walked away. The next farmhouse I came to was completely empty.

I continued traveling, and eventually came upon a gathering of American soldiers spread out in small groups. One of them gave me a slice of white bread. After eating the bread I became very ill. I lay down on the ground and groaned in pain. The soldiers summoned a truck and took me to where some of my former comrades had gathered. After a rest I was able to eat.

The Americans took us to an SS hospital, part of a mountain resort that had been turned into an SS rest and recreation facility. Until we arrived, only the SS elite had been fortunate enough to have been hospitalized there; the bathroom had marble sinks. General Eisenhower had ordered the SS to be removed from the resort and Jewish survivors to be sent there instead.

For us it was like living in a dream world. The faucets looked as if they were made of gold. Every imaginable convenience had been included, and we were expected to enjoy it as best we could. Dr. Grunwald appeared, quite recovered from his earlier ordeal, and was put in charge of our medical care.

Shortly after arriving at the resort, we gathered to discuss our situation. One of us, who we generally recognized as being the leader of our group said, "Although we are free, we must be careful with our lives. Seventy-five percent of us are very ill." We then held a memorial service for those who had perished in the camps. To us they were martyrs. The assembly was held in the courtyard, and the organizer was a Lithuanian Jew. He was a medical doctor and very religious. We recited the prayers in Hebrew, using a variation of Kaddish. The words went something like this:

"Blessed art thou, O Lord, our God, King of the Universe, Who hast saved a handful of the Jews, and liberated them from the Nazi murderers.

"Blessed art thou, O Lord, Our God, King of the Universe, Who hast kept us in life and has preserved us And enabled us to reach this season."

After the prayer, one of the group said "Nazi Germany, ruled by Hitler, lost the war as a nation, but they won the war against the Jews. They destroyed so many millions of people, their homes, and their culture. The German nation bears this responsibility as long as humans live on earth. They cannot wash Jewish blood from their souls and consciences. History has recorded that any nation that raised a sword against the Jews was paid back with destruction, with divine judgment, just as other nations were destroyed by God for the punishment of their sins."

After a month at the retreat, I was moved to a building that had housed SS members in Munich. All through the city, there was devastation. An American tank still contained the remains of its fighting crew, killed by the Germans. They had not yet reached their final resting place. The city was so full of rubble that bulldozers were needed just to clear walkways through the street.

By June of 1945, I was in the displaced persons camp at Feldafing, Germany. I was very sick and suffered from four open ulcers. Since 1943, when I had arrived at Blyzin, until June 1945, I had lived from day to day with painful cramps and bleeding ulcers. But even more, my heart was bleeding with the torturous news that I was the only member of my family left alive. Six others perished and no markers could be placed on their graves to honor their memories and names.

### Rachel

In November of 1939, Rachel was machine-gunned on the streets of Warsaw by the crew of a roving "volkswagen" jeep.

### Maurice

One day, towards the end of March in 1943, while in the Wolanow camp, I came back to our house from the air base and found my mother crying uncontrollably. She told me that she had just seen the Germans kill Morrie. Maurice had been doing some work in the main office in the camp and had been told to go into town to get a dictionary for the office. Having bought the dictionary, he stopped at a Christian home where he bought some bread. As he was riding his bicycle back to the camp he was stopped by the German gendarmes who searched him and found the bread. He told them that he had bought the bread, but it was illegal for Jews to buy and sell things to and from Christians. He was taken to the Wolanow police station where, along with two other Jewish men who worked in the camp office and who had been arrested after Morrie's interrogation, he spent the night.

The next day he and the others were sentenced to death. They were taken to an area outside the camp, and as they passed by a fence near the women's barracks he called out "Mama, Mama . . ." to our mother who was standing behind the barbed wire. She was crying out to him as she saw the gendarmes march him up to the edge of the mass grave off in the distance. She then heard shots and saw him fall into the grave.

### Nathan David

In October of 1944, Nathan David was taken away from Auschwitz, where he had been a transport kommando, to lower Bavaria, near the city of Linden, where he was forced to do hard physical labor. Some survivors of that labor camp told me that conditions there were terrible, similar to those in Kaufering. While Nathan David was there he developed a cold that became pneumonia. He ran a very high fever, and died.

### Father

My father was transported from Blizyn to a labor camp in Poland and then to Steinbrucken in Germany, where he worked in a quarry breaking up stones and rocks with a pick. A survivor told me that one day in January 1945, an SS man told my father that he wasn't working hard enough. He kicked my father so hard that he fell down the side of the quarry, rolling over and over as he hit the rocks. He died from the fall.

I was at Kaufering in January of 1945, and at about the same time that my father had his fatal fall I had a dream that I was walking in my father's funeral procession. The dream was so vivid that from that time on I was convinced that my father was dead and I mourned his passing.

### Mother

Mother was still in Auschwitz as the Russians approached. The Germans placed her in a transport destined for Bergen-Belsen. The train stopped first at Frankfurt where mother was placed in a cattle car with many young Russian and Polish prostitutes who had serviced the German, Ukrainian, and Hungarian troops, along with Jewish women from Auschwitz. As was the case in these transports, the cattle car was terribly crowded. In an attempt to make more room for themselves, the Russian women decided to kill as many of the Jews as possible. They began strangling the older Jewish women. Although some of the younger Jewish women fought with the Russians to prevent them from killing the weak and elderly, they could only save a few. My mother was among those who was choked to death. When the transport arrived at Bergen-Belsen she was taken out and buried in a large mass grave, the same one in which Anne Frank was buried.

*Toba*

Sometime after Toba left Auschwitz, she was placed in a transport that took her to Stettin, a port city on the Baltic. As the Russians approached, the Germans placed some 3,500 women prisoners in a transport ship. The vessel was taken out to sea and deliberately blown up, killing all the women on board. I learned this from a woman who arrived at Stettin too late to be placed on board and who was liberated by the Russians the next day.

◆ ◆ ◆

Day after day I walked to the edge of the Stabensea River, near Feldafing, trying to find answers to the questions the camps had posed for me. Why was our human race created and what was its mission on earth? Why had I survived when the whole world was corrupt? I felt as if no one cared about our suffering.

I returned to the barrack where I lived in a room with six other survivors, Jews, like myself. They didn't seem to think about the future. They kept busy cooking, washing, and eating. Several had contracted tuberculosis, and all of us had eye problems and emotional ones as well. Our teeth were in terrible condition, rotted with infection.

Most of the time, I felt as if life was not worth living, and I did not wish to go on. I was only 29. One day, I decided I would end my life, that I would drown myself. For me there would be no more suffering. I couldn't swim, so I knew that once I was in the water, I could not change my mind. I paused at the edge of the river and stared into the water below, thinking how quickly it would swallow me. Just as I was ready to jump, I saw my mother's face as she had looked as a young woman. She seemed to be walking in front of me, her voice ringing in my ears. I could hear her calling, "Kiwa, Kiwa, my child. Stop. I want to touch your hand." I became paralyzed, and I couldn't take another step. I did not know where I was. I was very confused.

In a short time I regained my senses. But I still felt her presence near me, and I could hear her voice clearly. I began to shiver and shake, and I broke into a sweat. I looked at the turbulent water below and asked myself what I was doing. I saw my mother stretch out her hand to save me. I sat down on the river bank and remembered what she had said to me across the barbed wire at Auschwitz, around the time of Rosh Hashonah in 1944. She said then that it was God's will that I would survive, and that Toba and Nathan David would also survive, and she prophesied that she and my father would perish and offer themselves for their children. The tears were washing down your beautiful face, mother, and you swallowed the salty tears. You said that all Jewish mothers had seen their children and families slaughtered like cattle in a slaughter house, the children whom they loved so dearly and who died in their innocence.

My dear mother, after the liberation, I had a concussion one morning and could hardly remember anything except your name and father's name and those of my brothers and sisters and very little about the rest of our large family. When I regained my memory, I didn't forget your wish, the last words we spoke with each other. As you know mother, I am the sole survivor, the only one left to tell our story.

*Carl Kiwa Rozenberg*

# SS personnel

*Obersturmbannführer*            Lieutenant Colonel

*Sturmbannführer*                Major

*Obersturmführer*                First Lieutenant

*Oberscharführer*                Technical Sergeant (NCO)


*Sicherheitsdienst (SD)*         Security Service

# glossary

| | |
|---|---|
| *Achtung* | Attention |
| *Blockälteste* | In charge of a barrack |
| *Cheder* | Hebrew school |
| *Kaddish* | Prayer for the dead |
| *Kapo* | Prisoner in charge of a work gang |
| *Kommando* | Work gang |
| *Lazaret* | Infirmary |
| *Minyan* | Quorum of ten adult Jewish males required for communal worship |
| *Mitzvah* | Divinely commanded good deed; charity is one such act |
| *Rosh Hashonah* | New Year |
| *Schneidermeister* | Master tailor |
| *Shiva* | Seven day period of mourning for a deceased member of a family |
| *Tallis* | Prayer shawl |
| *Tefillin* | Phylacteries |
| *Yarmulke* | Skull cap |
| *Yom Kippur* | Day of Atonement |